SLEEVES BLUSHER VEIL B

CHANTILLY LACE CH

UCHESSE SATIN EMPIRE WAIST

LLA PAGEANT BOUQUET PAILL

NG TIARA TRUMPET SKIRT TULL

RAIN BALL GOWN BATEAU NE

TLE CATHEDRAL TRAIN CHARM

LINE CRUMB CATCHER DUPIO

AN-BACK SKIRT JULIET SLEEVE

TTES PETAL SLEEVE RUCHING

E WATERFALL BOUQUET WATT

KLINE BELL SLEEVES BLUSHER

MEUSE CHANTILLY LACE CHIFF

UCHESSE SATIN EMPIRE WAIST

LLA PAGEANT BOUQUET PAILL

NG TIARA TRUMPET SKIRT TULL

*the knot* BOOK OF WEDDING GOWNS

# *the knot* BOOK OF
# WEDDING GOWNS

BY CARLEY RONEY

**CHRONICLE BOOKS**
SAN FRANCISCO

Library of Congress Cataloging-in-Publication Data:

Roney, Carley.
  The Knot book of wedding gowns / by Carley Roney.
      p. cm.

  ISBN 0-8118-3223-6

  1. Wedding costume. 2. Wedding costume—Purchasing. I. Knot (Firm) II. Title.

TT633 .R66 2001                          2001028032
392.5'4—dc21

Designed by Frances Baca
Illustrations by Amy Saidens
Printed in Hong Kong

Distributed in Canada by Raincoast Books
9050 Shaughnessy Street
Vancouver, British Columbia v6p 6e5

10 9 8 7 6 5 4 3 2 1

Chronicle Books LLC
85 Second Street
San Francisco, California 94105

www.chroniclebooks.com

ADDITIONAL PHOTOGRAPHS USED
COURTESY OF THE FOLLOWING:

© AP/WIDE WORLD PHOTOS: 15, 20, 25, 29

Cristina Tarantola: front cover, back cover,
back flap, 6, 102, 106 (top), 107 (top),
124 (top), 125 (top), 126, 136, 145, 153, 166

© Bettmann/CORBIS: 12, 16, 19, 21, 22, 23,
24, 26, 28

© Hulton-Deutsch Collection/CORBIS: 13

© Denis Reggie: 31

© Everett Collection: 17

Mark Loader: 138

© Musee du Temps, Besancon, France/
Bridgeman Art Library: 11

Nils Larsen: 148

Paul Costello: back cover (far left), 2, 105,
106 (bottom), 107 (bottom), 110, 111, 123,
124 (bottom), 125 (bottom), 129, 141, 146,
150, 154, 158

© Roy Miles Fine Paintings/Bridgeman Art
Library: 8

© TimePix: 27

# CONTENTS

Close your eyes and conjure it: the wedding gown. It's loaded with symbolism. It's laced with history. It has gone in and out of fashion. But what ultimately makes it the dress of all dresses is that it is a serious statement of personal style. Deliberated over for days, months even, and the focus of attention for so many, a bride's gown sends out a direct message about who she is to all who see her. And believe us, heads will turn! For this reason, we suspect the one burning question for every bride in the midst of the wedding planning process is, "What am I going to wear?" Maybe you've had a dress in mind since you were a kid, or maybe you're one of those who don't have a clue. Either way, welcome to the shopping trip of a lifetime.

A wedding gown is the most special—and, we should point out, perhaps the most costly—dress you'll ever wear. But before you start to feel overwhelmed, there's no need to have a clothing crisis. Though there are thousands of gowns out there, you can find your ideal with a simple understanding of the elements of a wedding gown and how they come together. That's where this book comes in. In Chapter Two, you'll discover a whole new vocabulary of gown terms (it's fun, we promise—ever heard of a crumb catcher?) with illustrations to help you understand how the bodice affects the waistline, which in turn determines the silhouette.

In Chapter Three, you'll identify your bridal personality and get ready for your first forays into the world of bridal salons and trunk shows. Are you a princess or a bohemian? A romantic or a minimalist? It all comes down to knowing thyself, thy budget, and thy seasonal and religious restrictions.

In Chapter Four we talk accessories. Do you need the headpiece, veil, jewelry, gloves, handbag, wrap, *and* the garter? Maybe not. But you do need to know what your options are, and the role these accoutrements play in your overall look. And while your bridesmaids and your groom are not accessories per se, you wouldn't get married without them (especially the groom), so we've included some guidelines for figuring out how they, too, can complement your style.

As for the day to say "I do," Chapter Five helps you pull it all together, from the moment you step out of bed to the moment your groom helps you out of your gown. What goes in your emergency bridal kit? Who bustles your train after the ceremony? We've thought of all the things you may not have, so commit these wedding-day details to memory for smooth sailing.

Now, ready to go shopping? Not so fast. First, Chapter One—a little history lesson.

# ANCIENT TIMES

## CEREMONIOUS

This Pre-Raphaelite painting by Alcide Theophile Robaudi, entitled *THE YOUNG BRIDE*, depicts a young woman in classical wedding garb. She wears long, pleated white robes, a modest soft yellow veil, and strings of pearls—the oldest-known gem and a symbol of purity and perfection.

In ancient Egypt, brides were traditionally draped in layers of pleated white linen. In Greece, white was the color of celebration and therefore generally worn for weddings as an emblem of joy. At Roman weddings, brides donned softly pleated white robes as a tribute to Hymen, the god of fertility and marriage, who was said to have particularly admired the color white. And, in what must have been a shocking visual contrast, both Greek and Roman brides covered their heads with flame-colored veils as a sign of modesty.

# 1500s to 1600s
## ROYAL TRADITION

One of the first officially documented white-wearing brides was Anne of Brittany, who married Louis XII of France in 1499. Margaret Tudor, the daughter of Henry VII, was married four years later in a white damask gown edged with crimson, the traditional color of royalty. And in 1612, when Princess Elizabeth, daughter of King James I, was married, it was in a silver dress embroidered with pearls, real silver, and precious stones. Since only royalty and the affluent could afford the luxury of a specially made wedding gown, however, most commoners—including those of the American colonies— simply donned their "Sunday best" dress to get married. Or, if they did have the means to make a special dress, they selected fabrics in soft blues, grays, pastels, and browns—in any shade except green, which was considered unlucky—that could easily fit into their everyday wardrobes.

This detail of the 17th-century *Charles V Tapestry* illustrates his marriage to ISABELLA OF PORTUGAL in 1526. The bride appears in a bejeweled gown richly embroidered in red and gold thread, a luxurious garment befitting her royal stature.

# 1800s
## LUXURIOUS

Throughout the eighteenth century and the first half of the nineteenth, royal brides for the most part remained true to luxurious fabrics in tones of silver and red, and the commoners to more subdued but still elegant dresses in various colors and floral patterns. Then, in 1840, along came Queen Victoria in her all-white bridal ensemble: Her rich white satin gown was adorned with orange blossoms and had an eighteen-foot train, which she carried over her arm. On her head, she wore a matching wreath of blossoms entwined with diamonds and a veil of Honiton lace. She was immediately heralded for her grace and beauty, and was ultimately responsible for establishing the white, worn-only-once gown as the Western wedding-day ideal. The manifestation of this ideal was helped along by the growing affluence of the times, which was creating larger middle and upper-middle classes that could afford such luxury. American women continued to take their cue from English and French fashions, especially from Worth of Paris, the most influential clothing designer of the time. Mid-century Civil War brides necessarily resorted to wearing their best dress, until post-war industrialization heralded a new era of prosperity, when brides could once again exult in the heavy decoration and dramatic trains of the bustled dresses of the day.

Left: QUEEN VICTORIA OF ENGLAND, at her marriage to Prince Albert in 1840, broke with royal tradition and wore a resplendent white satin gown trimmed with orange blossoms and yards of delicate Honiton lace, thereby popularizing the white wedding gown for generations to come. Above: Not wanting to miss out on the trend, THE DUCHESS OF ALBANY emulated Queen Victoria's bridal attire, donning white silk, orange blossoms, and a flowing veil in her 1882 wedding to Leopold, the Duke of Albany.

# 1900s
## PROPER

At the start of the twentieth century, brides were still experiencing the pressures of the prim and proper Victorian style of white gowns with long sleeves, ethereal floor-length veils, and the high necklines known as wedding-band collars. For the first time, clothing manufacturers produced elaborate, ready-made wedding gowns for a growing and socially conscious middle class. All of this was soon to change, however, in 1914, the year World War I began. Boned corsets were on their way out, as silhouettes loosened, emancipating women from the constricting garments of the past.

ELEANOR AND FRANKLIN D. ROOSEVELT were married on March 17, 1905. Her Victorian-style dress reflected the modesty of the times: stiff, heavy satin and shirred tulle, with a high neck, long sleeves, and a cinched waist.

# 1920s
## INNOVATION

In the early 1920s, changes in the social fiber that had begun during World War I forever altered the status of women in America, who were fighting against their traditional roles. The Nineteenth Amendment had given them the right to vote. Now, they were celebrating their freedom by cutting their hair into flirty bobs, wearing their dresses shorter and looser, and happily abandoning their restrictive corsets. High-society ladies still turned to Paris for their fashions, and it was during this time that Jeanne Lanvin and Coco Chanel rose to the top; the latter introduced the first official knee-length wedding gown, though it was done up in traditional bridal fabrics and accompanied with a full veil and a court train. It became the most popular wedding dress style, ushering in the decade of the flapper bride.

Left: Opera impresario Oscar Hammerstein II wed DOROTHY BLANCHARD on May 14, 1929, in a second marriage for both. The bride was elegant in her simple gray suit with fur-trimmed cape and cloche, sans veiling. Above: Brides of the 1920s relished the looser silhouettes and shortened hemlines of the era. Actress RUTH TAYLOR models the popular look, which was accompanied with dramatic flowing veils and long trains.

# 1930s
## SLEEK SOPHISTICATION

In 1930s America, the frivolity of the flapper era gave way to the Great Depression. It was a dark, difficult time, and wedding dresses reflected the new solemnity. Elaborate knee-length gowns with expensive embellishments were replaced by slim, unadorned, bias-cut floor-length silk dresses. Men and women alike retreated to the film fantasies churned out by the budding stars of Hollywood, whose influence grew with the rebounding economy at the end of the decade. American designers rose to prominence as a result of their film work, and they began creating sleek and modern gowns that mimicked the glamour and romance of Tinseltown. Also of note at the end of the decade was the introduction of synthetic fabrics in 1938, which were embraced by designers and consumers alike for their lower cost and versatility. With the Depression behind them, brides once again showed no restraint when it came to wedding ensembles, using as much lace, brocade, and silk as they wished.

King Edward VIII abdicated his throne to marry American divorcee WALLIS SIMPSON in France on June 3, 1937. The Duchess wore a floor-length silk crepe gown by Mainbocher in a soft blue hue dubbed "Wallis Blue." A pink-and-blue feathered hat crowned her head.

# 1940s
## REFINED STYLE

Just when things were looking up, on the heels of the Depression era came World War II. Both men and women went to war, the manufacture of superfluous items was halted, and strict rationing became the status quo. The war restrictions necessarily affected the fashions of the times, and that included bridal wear. Imports from abroad were restricted, so the scarcity of all kinds of fabric during wartime led to innovative wedding choices: It became the norm for brides to marry in their best suits or simple street clothes rather than full wedding regalia. Of course, with engagements lasting only days or weeks (before new husbands were shipped abroad), there wasn't much time to plan for a wedding gown anyway. The other acceptable wartime alternative? Borrowing a traditional white gown from friends or family members, or renting one.

Left: Despite wartime restrictions, a glimpse of opulence could still be seen in the wedding of the wealthy, including that of seventeen-year-old heiress GLORIA VANDERBILT, who married Pasquale DiCicco in a relatively lavish white satin gown in December 1941. Above: RITA HAYWORTH kept it simple at her May 1949 wedding to Aly Khan in France, wearing a belted white suit with a pleated skirt and a tulle-covered, wide-brimmed picture hat.

Above: At her 1956 wedding to Prince Rainier of Monaco, GRACE KELLY became a princess the moment she stepped into her exquisite ivory peau de soie and satin wedding gown embellished with yards of antique rose-point Brussels lace. Designed by Helen Rose of MGM Studios, the gown featured a ten-foot train, a molded bodice, a tiny waist, and the elaborate styling that was so popular at the time. Right: Already a fashion icon, AUDREY HEPBURN epitomized 1950s bridal style in this slim-waisted, cocktail-length wedding dress; on her head she wore a simple floral wreath. Hepburn and Mel Ferrer were wed on September 25, 1954.

# 1950s
## ICONIC ELEGANCE

The postwar 1950s were a time of celebration and prosperity. As such, the traditional Cinderella bridal gown created in the nineteenth century was reborn, and wedding dresses became bigger and more elaborate than ever. Waistlines were tiny, leading into billowing skirts at cocktail length. Nylon became a postwar fashion phenomenon, and designers began crafting crinolines, bridal veils, and dress fabrics from stiff nylon net. As such, 1950s brides often married in full but trainless white gowns made of nylon lace over stiff crinolines, with tight molded bodices and defined waists, and topped off with a short bouffant veil. Influential designers of the decade included Balenciaga and Givenchy in France, and America's own Claire McCardell, all of whom contributed to the air of sophistication and good taste prevalent during this period.

# 1960s
## FORMAL FREEDOM

For the greater part of the 1960s, formal wedding gowns prevailed. The most popular designs were longer versions of the same full-skirt, fitted-bodice styles favored in the 1950s. In the last few years of the decade, however, anti-war, pro-peace, pro-love young couples began to revolt, eschewing the long-standing bridal traditions of their parents' generation in favor of more simple ceremonies and freedom of expression. Many brides bid adieu to tulle and lace and instead chose cotton caftans and peasant smocks to say their "I dos." The year 1967 even saw dresses made out of paper, in keeping with a short-lived fad of disposable clothing!

Left: The 1967 nuptials of Elvis Presley and PRISCILLA BEAULIEU took place in a civil ceremony in Las Vegas. In true sixties style, the bride wore a loose-fitting, floor-length Empire gown with beaded bodice and a full fountain-style veil perched on her bouffant. The King wore a brocade tuxedo jacket befitting his pop-culture status. Above: MIA FARROW capitalized on the ever-shortening hemlines of the decade by selecting a mod two-piece suit in which to marry Frank Sinatra in July 1966. The skirt fell coquettishly to the knees, and Farrow left her pixie hairstyle unadorned.

Left: In 1977, tennis great Arthur Ashe's bride, **JEANNE MOUTOUSSAMY**, wore a modest, high-necked sheath, with lace edging around the neckline, cuffs, and hem. The look was simple and romantic.  Right: **BIANCA JAGGER** epitomized a woman's freedom to express her sexuality in the 1970s when she donned a fabulously sexy, skin-baring Yves Saint Laurent suit with a plunging neckline to wed Mick Jagger in 1971. A rose-trimmed, wide-brimmed hat topped off her daring look.

# SEXY SIMPLICITY
# 1970s

An expressive style continued throughout much of the 1970s, as newly liberated women emphatically broke with the demure traditions of the past. For the first time, women could choose the kind of bride they wanted to be: The decade saw everything from traditional ruffles and lace to miniskirts and trousers. The modern bride of the seventies embraced her sexuality, so much so that a white suit with an open jacket revealing bare skin became acceptable bridal attire.

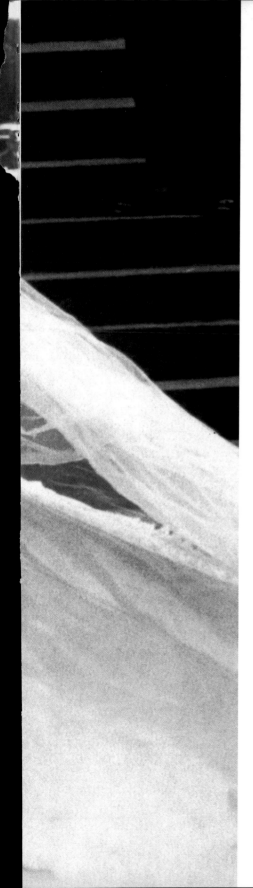

# 1980s

## FAIRY TALES

In 1981, when Lady Diana Spencer married Prince Charles of England, the world was reminded how truly romantic full bridal regalia could be. Princess Di was resplendent in a taffeta gown trimmed with thousands of sequins and pearls, antique lace, and a vast twenty-five-foot train. Suddenly, legions of brides wanted gowns fit for royalty, complete with trains and jeweled veils. Not surprisingly, the big white gown came back into style with a vengeance—the more layers and adornment, the better. Enter designer Vera Wang, whose ball gowns epitomized the princess bride.

Left: The gown worn by **LADY DIANA SPENCER** at her July 1981 wedding to Prince Charles had an effect similar to the one worn by her royal predecessor, Queen Victoria: It shifted our vision of proper bridal attire for the time, and was copied the world over. The fairy-tale silk taffeta ball gown, designed by Elizabeth and David Emanuel, was beyond sumptuous. Her long silk tulle veil was held in place by the Spencer-family diamond tiara. Above: The Kennedy clan was America's answer to royalty, and **CAROLINE KENNEDY** its princess. When she wed Edwin Schlossberg in 1986, Caroline turned to designer Carolina Herrera to create her lavish satin organza gown. In a nod to Kennedy's Irish heritage, Herrera embellished the gown with hundreds of four-leaf-clover appliqués.

# 1990s
## UNADORNED BEAUTY

By the time the 1990s rolled around, the excesses and ostentatious displays of wealth that characterized the 1980s were dwindling in popularity. Ditto the superfluously ornate bridal gown. Instead, wedding dresses in the nineties were characterized by their sensual, uncomplicated shapes and styles. Later in the decade, sleek A-lines and sheaths became popular, as did shorter gowns, splashes of color, and pantsuits—not to mention the slip dress, which became a viable wedding gown option overnight when Carolyn Bessette wore one to marry John F. Kennedy Jr. By the end of the decade, one thing was clear: More than ever, a bride's choice of gown reflected her own unique personality.

In September 1996, it was John F. Kennedy Jr.'s turn to get married. His bride was CAROLYN BESSETTE, and she introduced the world to the slip dress as wedding gown. Narciso Rodriguez designed the pearl-colored bias-cut silk crepe gown, which Carolyn wore with a tulle veil, sheer elbow-length gloves, and beaded strappy sandals. Her unadorned yet sexy look was captured by Denis Reggie in a photograph reproduced around the world.

# TODAY
## BLENDING OLD & NEW

As we settle into the new millennium, bridal fashion can only be described as an exciting blend of old and new, of classic design and daring detail. There is indeed something for everyone, be it a body-skimming gown with a bare back for the true vixen; an ethereal A-line with diaphanous layers for the bohemian; an asymmetrical ensemble for the bold minimalist; or a strapless gown with a full tulle skirt for the consummate princess.

Gowns are also getting a boost of freshness and fun from whimsical embellishment and sprinklings of color. Fabrics are adorned with everything from pink, blue, and platinum embroideries to sparkling crystal droplets, lace appliqués, and whisper-soft feathers and fur. The choices are endless. And while some of today's shapes are a far cry from dresses worn at the turn of the previous century, in the end, even the most cutting-edge gown is steeped in tradition. How? As long as you're wearing white, you're contributing to the continuity of custom. Congratulations—you can now take your place in wedding-gown history.

As bridalwear designers look forward, they continue to discover inspiration in the past. For Spring 2001 at JIM HJELM COUTURE, designer NATASHA ADONZIO showed an antique duchesse satin A-line gown (above) with an Empire bodice, coupled with a medieval-style headband and long flowing veil. And in a fabulously futuristic finale, ADONZIO crafted a one-of-a-kind peach-colored duchesse satin gown (left) with a hi-lo hoop overskirt, for the truly fashion-forward.

SILHOUETTE  Ball gown

NECKLINE  Square

LACE  French lace overlay

BODICE  Fitted bodice in duchesse satin with French lace overlay and front panel with double boning and beading.

WAISTLINE  Drop waist

SKIRT  Floor length with side-seam pleating

TRAIN  Sweep

FABRIC  Silk gazar

# 2 | ANATOMY

**Though** you might consider your gown a single element, it is actually the sum of specific components. Singly, these parts create certain visual effects and flatter your figure. Together, they unite to express your individual style and form your perfect gown. For starters, look at a gown in terms of its overall silhouette—big and poufy, sleek and slender, or somewhere in between—and decide which appeals to you the most. This first decision should be the clearest; all the other parts will come into focus once you head out to the salons. You will probably be confused at first, so our best advice is to use this chapter to learn the basic details of gown construction. That way, you'll be able to make the rest of your decisions knowing what to look for and what suits you best.

# SILHOUETTE

*Silhouette* refers to the overall cut of a gown. It's the most essential element to focus on, because a gown's shape is its bedrock—it's what sets the mood for the entire garment. The fitted bodice and full bell-shaped skirt of the ball gown, for example, has the presence of a princess. More form-fitting styles, like the A-line and sheath, offer a different appeal: The former elongates the lines of the body, adding a classic elegance and the illusion of length, while the latter ups the ante on wedding-dress sex appeal, creating a sleek and modern option for the dare-to-be-more-bare bride.

## BALL GOWN

Depending on the fabric of the skirt, a ball gown can take many different shapes.

FIGURE 1    This ball gown skirt of silk mikado with box pleats offers a more structured silhouette with a regal sheen.

FIGURE 2    Silk tulle and lace imbue this ball gown with weightless romance.

FIGURE 3    A ball gown skirt in tulle is soft, ethereal, and full, but without a lot of weight.

FIGURE 4    This ball gown of silk peau de soie is fuller, with a more dramatic luster.

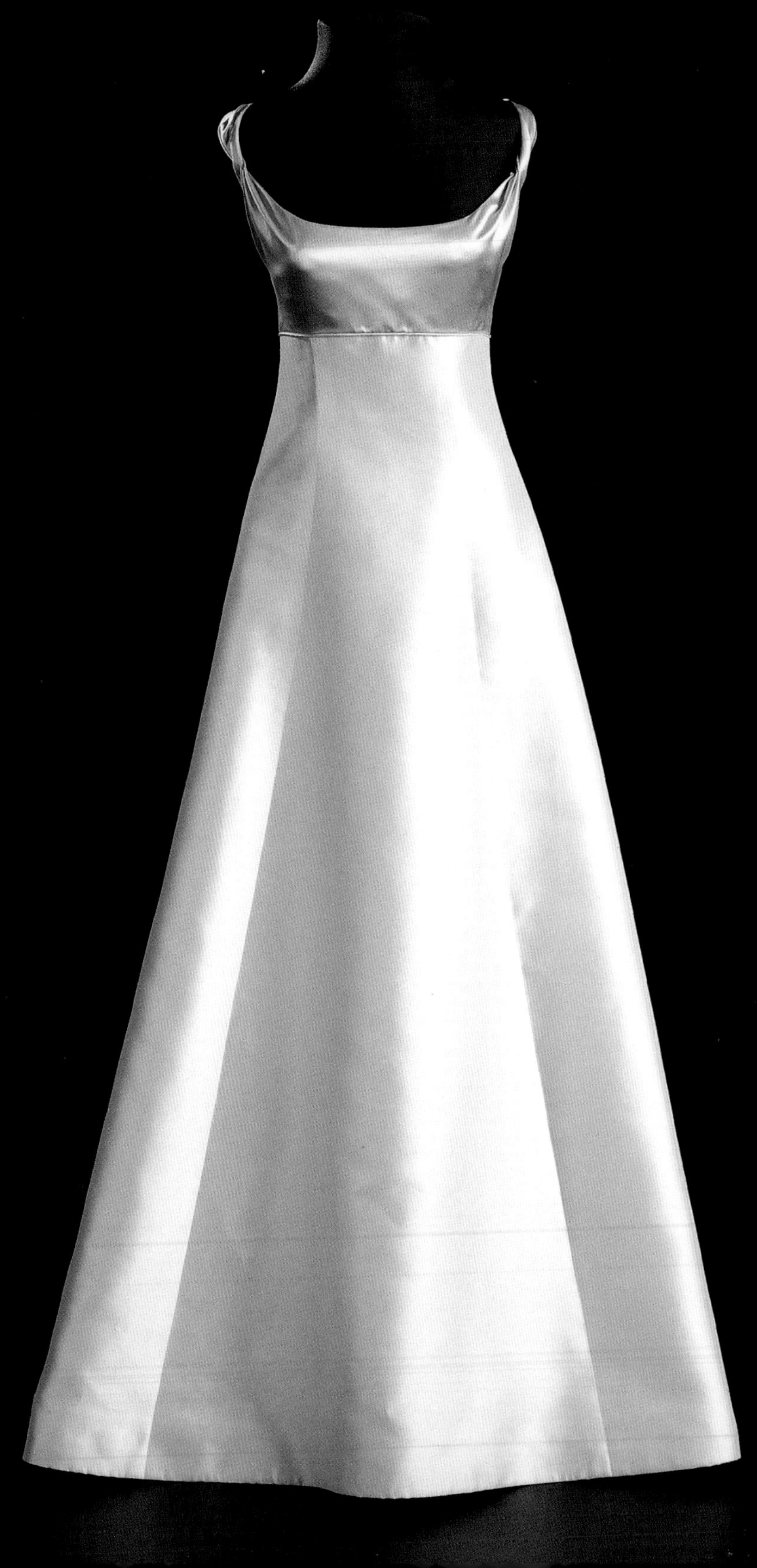

# A-LINE
# SILHOUETTE

A-line gowns have an A-shape, created by vertical seams running from the shoulders to a flared skirt, and are characterized by their narrow-at-the-top, wider-at-the-bottom shape. But there are a number of versions that produce varied effects on the frame, depending on the fullness of the skirt and the weight of the fabric.

FIGURE 5   A satin and silk mikado gown with a sexy scoop neck is seasonless, with a wonderfully rich surface luster.

FIGURE 6   A V-neck A-line gown in silk organza is crisp and lightweight, gracefully echoing the body's natural curves.

FIGURE 7   An Empire-waist A-line gown in silk peau de soie is heavier in weight but wonderfully soft and matte.

FIGURE 8   A strapless A-line with a notched neckline in embroidered satin-faced organza is bare and lightweight, though the fabric lends a crisp appearance.

# SHEATH
# SILHOUETTE

A sheath offers a slim profile that closely
follows the curves of the body. Sheaths can
be super-slim or long and flowing, depending
on the drape and cut of the fabric.

FIGURE 9   A sweep-train sheath in four-
ply silk and silk chiffon is very lightweight and
fluid, with a drapey weave and matte finish.

FIGURE 10   A sheath with an embroidered
silk organza overlay is both lightweight
and ethereal.

FIGURE 11   A strapless, mermaid-cut
sheath in leather is dramatically body-skimming
for the ultimate in sex appeal.

FIGURE 12   A silk mikado sheath with a
belted waist and bolero jacket is both lustrous
and seasonless, thanks to its medium weight
and finely spun fibers.

9 | 10

| 11

BALL GOWN            SHEATH            A-LINE

THE BALL GOWN   The most traditional of all shapes, the ball gown is typified by a fitted bodice and natural or dropped waistline that leads to a very full skirt. Pleats or gathers in the skirt are what make it a ball gown. GOOD FOR: skinny minnies (adds curves) and pear shapes (the skirt hides *everything*). BAD FOR: the petite among us (the excess fabric can overwhelm tiny frames) and those with a lot on top (you might end up looking round).

THE SHEATH   A modern, sexier take on the traditional wedding gown, the sheath is characterized by a slim profile that closely follows the curves of the body. GOOD FOR: the tall and thin as well as the slim and petite (the lean shape adds length). BAD FOR: anyone who feels like they have something to hide (we repeat: lean shape).

THE A-LINE   As its name implies, the A-line cut is narrow at the top, cut close to the ribcage, and extends out along the body in the shape of a triangle (or "A") in a smooth, elongated line. It is perhaps the most popular skirt option, as it looks wonderful on a variety of body types. The lines of the skirt are always clean and ungathered, but there is, as always, a number of versions. The princess cut is exemplified by vertical seams traveling from the bust to the hem. Another take is the circle skirt, a very wide A-line with a full skirt. GOOD FOR: most body types. BAD FOR: almost no one.

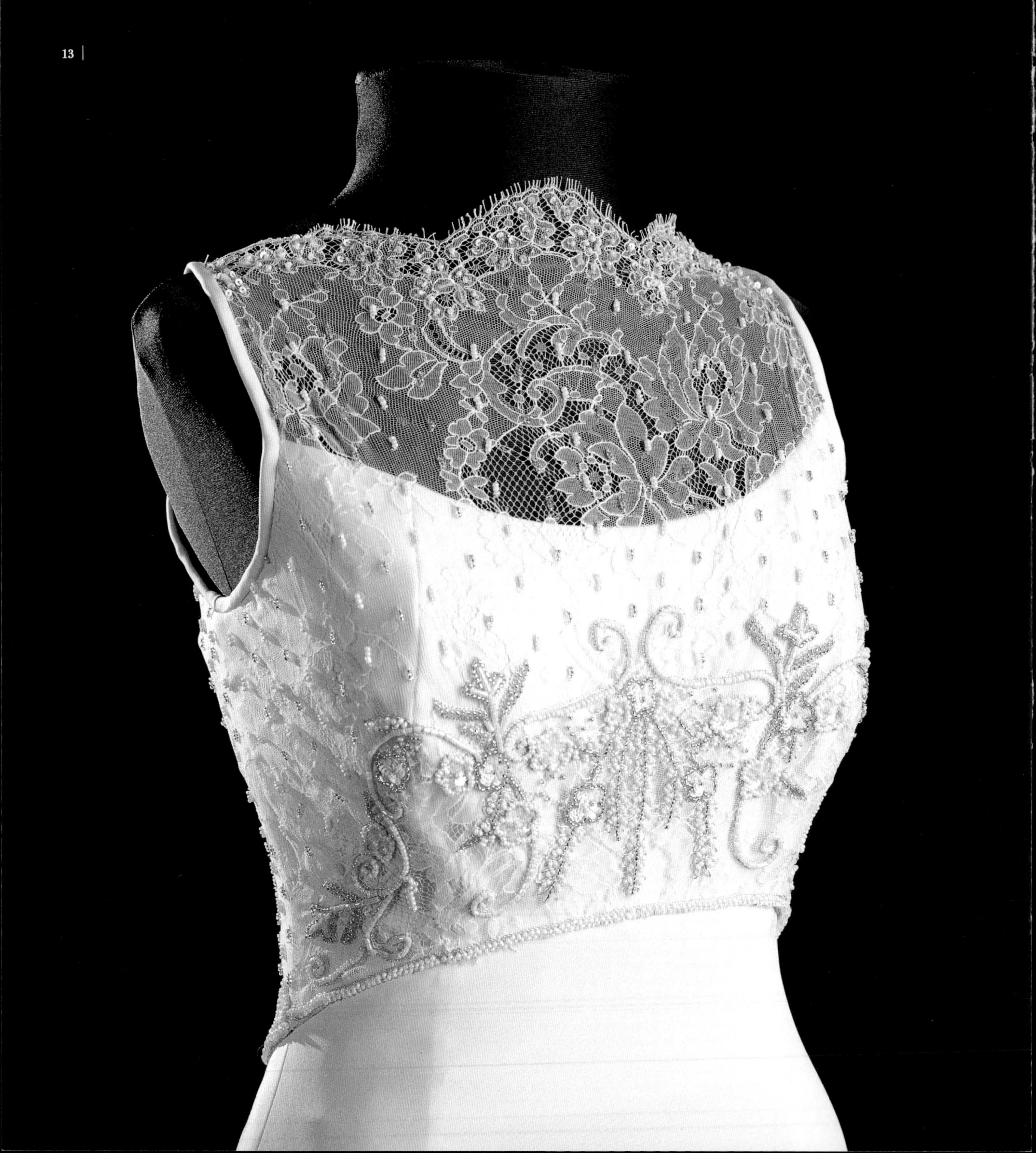

# BODICE

The bodice is the upper portion of the gown structured around the ribcage. It essentially covers the bosom and back, and includes the neckline and the waistline. The most precise measurements taken for a gown center around the fit of the bodice, which, more than any other part of the dress, should fit perfectly. The bodice can be shaped by simple seaming or darts, or by more elaborate concealed boning or a seductive laced-corset construction. Often, the bodice is where beading, embroidery, or other embellishments play a major role in a gown's design.

FIGURE 13 A sheer Chantilly lace overlay adds romance to a silk crepe gown; the extra whisper of fabric beautifully highlights the face and neck.

FIGURE 14 Extensive boning helps mold the bodice of a duchesse satin ball gown.

FIGURE 15 A lace-up corset back adds seduction and romance to a ball gown, and draws attention to a small waist.

FIGURE 16 A lace and crystal-encrusted insert at the neckline of this pleated ball gown draws the eye upward, giving the illusion of added height.

FIGURE 17 Floral appliqués and a touch of draping add dimension and whimsy to the bodice of a silk taffeta princess-line gown.

15 | 16

| 17

CRUMB CATCHER

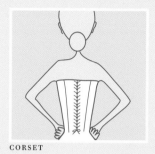

BONING

CORSET

KEYHOLE

OVERLAY

RUCHING

INSERT

CRUMB CATCHER   An insert of fabric at the bust creates a double-layered effect; the one closest to the body is fitted, while the other protrudes slightly.

BONING   Stays used in corset and strapless bodices for shaping and stiffening.

CORSET   A tight, figure-enhancing bodice that laces up the back.

KEYHOLE   A wedge- or keyhole-shaped cutout in a high, round neckline.

OVERLAY   A piece of fabric—usually sheer—layered on top of the main fabric.

RUCHING   An application of fabric that is gathered at two ends via concealed strings.

INSERT   A piece of fabric, usually of contrasting texture, inserted between pieces of the main fabric of the gown.

# NECKLINE

The neckline is probably the feature brides focus on most after the shape. Not only is it the part of the dress people spend the most time looking at, but it's also the one that draws attention to the face, the collarbone, and the décolletage. Some necklines—the bateau, jewel, and high collar—sit high on, or even cover, the collarbone. Others—the portrait, sweetheart, scoop, keyhole, and strapless—are defined by what they leave bare. Because of its prominence, many brides rely on the neckline to add character to a gown, to show off an accessory, or to highlight a unique figure feature, be it a long, graceful neck, a daring décolletage, or strong shoulders.

FIGURE 18 A French embroidered duchesse satin halter shows off strong shoulders and a sexy back.

FIGURE 19 A lacy sweetheart neckline is perfect for accentuating décolletage.

FIGURE 20 A sheer tulle scoop neckline flatters most body types, as it shows off the neck and dips into the chest without being too revealing.

FIGURE 21 A bateau neckline in silk satin is classic and timeless, and great for women who are smaller on top.

18

19

20

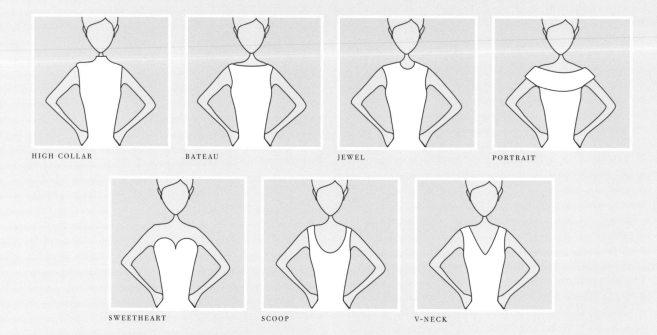

HIGH COLLAR    BATEAU    JEWEL    PORTRAIT

SWEETHEART    SCOOP    V-NECK

HIGH COLLAR  A band collar that extends up the neck. The mandarin version of this style is taken from traditional Asian dress, and doesn't quite meet at the center front. GOOD FOR: just about anyone desiring an elongated effect; very flattering with an updo. BAD FOR: those with a wider neck, where the fit may be too snug.

BATEAU  This wide-necked shape follows the curve of the collarbone, almost to the tip of the shoulders. The *Sabrina* version—made popular by actress Audrey Hepburn—is sleeveless; the front and back panels just touch at the shoulders, sometimes with thin straps. GOOD FOR: the bony and the flat chested (boosts the bust). BAD FOR: brides on the busty side (ditto).

JEWEL  Also known as the T-shirt neckline, the jewel neckline is round and sits at the base of the throat. GOOD FOR: the flat chested (makes you bustier) and the collar-bone conscious (hides deep hollows). BAD FOR: the larger breasted (makes you bustier).

PORTRAIT  Characterized by a wide, soft scoop from shoulder to shoulder. GOOD FOR: great collarbones (shows them off). BAD FOR: undefined or bony collarbones .

SWEETHEART  A low-cut neckline shaped like the top half of a heart, accentuating the décolletage. Often done with an overlay of sheer material that rises higher, elongating the torso and neck. GOOD FOR: serious cleavage (a tasteful display). BAD FOR: the décolletage-impaired.

SCOOP  Also known as a ballerina neckline, this U-shaped style can be cut low, and quite often the scoop will continue on the back of the dress. GOOD FOR: everyone.

V-NECK  The neckline dips down in the front in a flattering V, elongating the neckline and de-emphasizing the bustline. GOOD FOR: B or C cups. BAD FOR: anything smaller or larger (the bodice will either seem too empty or too full).

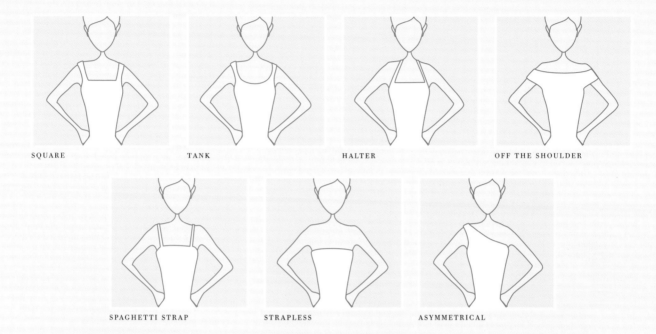

SQUARE · TANK · HALTER · OFF THE SHOULDER

SPAGHETTI STRAP · STRAPLESS · ASYMMETRICAL

SQUARE  The name makes it obvious: The neckline is cut straight across the front. GOOD FOR: the bust-endowed (cuts low but is not revealing). BAD FOR: almost no one.

TANK  Similar to a men's undershirt, with a U-shaped neckline and deep armholes under the shoulders and narrow straps. GOOD FOR: brides with buff arms. BAD FOR: those with arm issues.

HALTER  The halter features straps that wrap around the neck, or a high neck with deep armholes. Sometimes backless. GOOD FOR: great shoulders. BAD FOR: broad or narrow shoulders; anyone who needs the support of a bra.

OFF THE SHOULDER  This neckline sits below the shoulders, with sleevelike straps that cover part of the upper arm. Shows off your collarbone and shoulders. GOOD FOR: medium- or full-chested women (open-neck styling with the support of straps); pear shapes. BAD FOR: broad shoulders (accentuates the obvious) and thin hips.

SPAGHETTI STRAP  This neckline is nearly strapless, save for the presence of thin, delicate straps. GOOD FOR: small to medium breasts. BAD FOR: large breasts or broad shoulders.

STRAPLESS  This bodice is usually cut straight across, but it can also peak on the sides or have a slight dip in the center. GOOD FOR: broad or thick shoulders. BAD FOR: smaller chests (unless you're wearing a push-up bra).

ASYMMETRICAL  This neckline appears different on either side of the center front; one example is a one-shoulder design. GOOD FOR: great collarbones; the bra-free. BAD FOR: the bra-dependent; those with broad shoulders.

22 | 23

24 | 25

# WAISTLINE

Technically, the waistline of the wedding dress is the horizontal seam that joins the bodice and skirt. Along with the neckline and sleeves, the waistline works to add signature style to a particular silhouette. It's also the element responsible for bringing shape and balance to the gown. For example, the elongated V-shape of a Basque waist beautifully reins in a full ball gown, while the natural waist on an A-line dress will subtly highlight the gentle curve of the design. Waistlines can also be used to manipulate gown proportion. Dropped waists, which came to prominence during the flapper era, help create the illusion of a longer torso, while high Empire-style waists are favored for their slimming properties.

FIGURE 22   An Empire waist on a gown of beaded silk crepe and silk georgette lends a period look and de-emphasizes a thick waist.

FIGURE 23   A natural waist on a silk satin organza and duchesse satin A-line gown highlights the curves of the wearer's figure.

FIGURE 24   A princess line on a strapless gown creates the illusion of elongation using vertical seams.

FIGURE 25   A duchesse satin ball gown with a Basque waist slims the waistline and de-emphasizes hips.

FIGURE 26   The dropped waist on an Italian silk satin A-line gown hits below the navel, emphasizing a tiny waist.

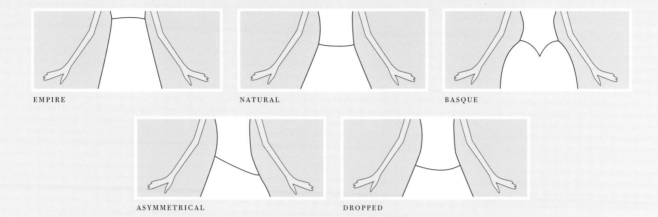

EMPIRE     NATURAL     BASQUE

ASYMMETRICAL     DROPPED

EMPIRE   The Empire features a high-waisted seam just below the bustline; the skirt falls in a slight A-line. Named after the style's popularity during the Empire period in France. GOOD FOR: brides with a smaller bust (adds emphasis); the waist-minimizing cut allows extra room for brides who have tummy issues or are pregnant. BAD FOR: brides with a well-endowed bust (may make you appear top-heavy) or full hips.

NATURAL   The seam of this waistline lies, as the name implies, at the natural waist, which is the indentation between the hip and the ribcage. GOOD FOR: almost everyone. BAD FOR: anyone thicker around the middle.

BASQUE   The Basque waist forms an elongated triangle beneath your own natural waistline. This style diminishes the width of the dress at the waist. GOOD FOR: full or hourglass figures or those seeking less emphasis on the hips. BAD FOR: problem bellies.

ASYMMETRICAL   An asymmetrical bodice features a change in waist height from one side of the dress to the other. The extent to which this style flatters certain figures may vary, depending on the cut.

DROPPED   The dropped waist falls several inches below your natural waistline. GOOD FOR: elongating the torso. BAD FOR: those with narrow shoulders (gives you an A shape) or long waists (adds extra length).

# SLEEVES

Wedding-dress sleeves can add interest to a bodice and provide balance for a skirt. Once closely linked to season, the selection of sleeve style is now largely a matter of how much—or how little—skin the wearer is willing (or allowed) to show. Both options can be equally dramatic. Long-sleeved styles designed for maximum flair include the Juliet (as in *Romeo and . . .*), a long, fitted sleeve with a short puff at the shoulder; and the bell, a sleeve narrow at the armhole and then wide at the wrist. On the other end of the spectrum are alluring super-spare styles such as the petal and the cap, both of which offer just enough material to cover the shoulder. Sleeves don't have to be made from the same opaque fabric as the gown; often they are made of tulle, lace, or illusion netting, which create a "barely there" effect even when the sleeves are long.

FIGURE 27  Three-quarter-length silk organza sleeves are a great modern option for the bride who desires diaphanous arm coverage.

FIGURE 28  The T-shirt sleeve is a classic look for the conservative bride, but this sheer organza version is sexier and more modern.

FIGURE 29  Off-the-shoulder silk-faced satin cap sleeves are sturdy and opaque, yet super-sexy.

FIGURE 30  Double organza cap sleeves, which offer just enough material to shield the shoulder, have delicate puffs of fabric with a "barely there" effect.

FIGURE 31  This embroidered matte satin gown features a longer version of the T-shirt sleeve for added coverage.

27 | 28

| 29

| 30

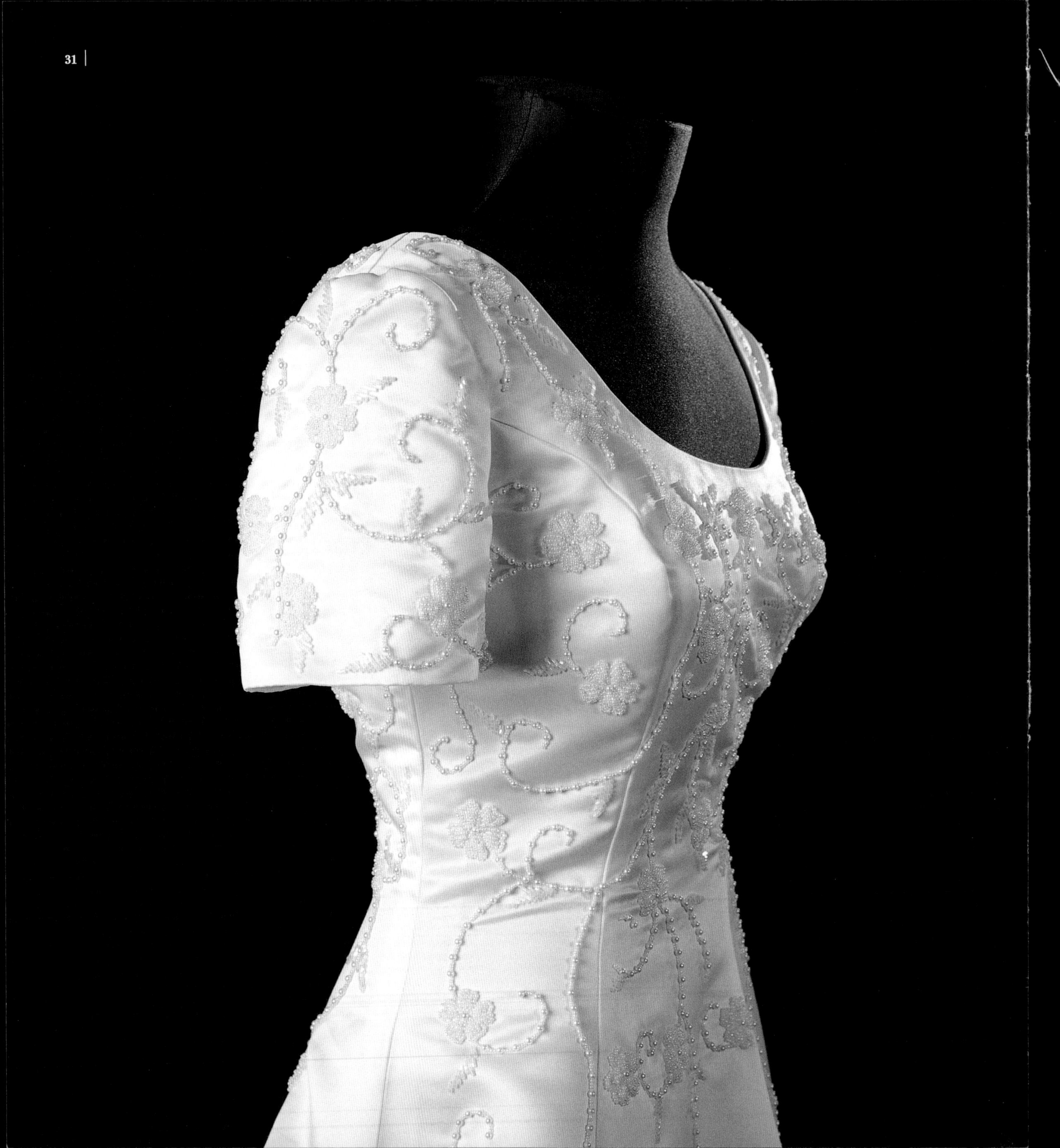

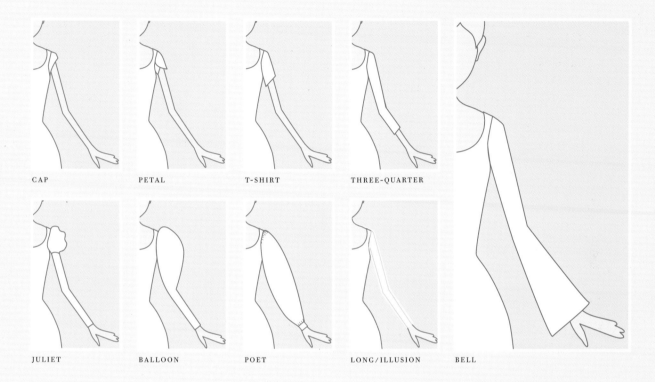

CAP     PETAL     T-SHIRT     THREE-QUARTER

JULIET     BALLOON     POET     LONG/ILLUSION     BELL

CAP   A small sleeve, shorter and more rounded than a T-shirt sleeve, covering just the shoulder. Best on women with fairly slender or well-toned upper arms.

PETAL   A short sleeve that criss-crosses over the bicep of the arm. Also known as the tulip sleeve.

T-SHIRT   As the name indicates, these sleeves look like those on your favorite T-shirt—a good option for brides who want to cover their upper arms. If you're self-conscious about baring your triceps/biceps, this option may be for you.

THREE-QUARTER   Ending midway between the elbow and the wrist, this sleeve style has made a big comeback in the fashion world. It's an elegant look in bridalwear: cool, yet covered.

JULIET   A long sleeve with a short puff at the shoulder that's fitted on the lower part of the arm. Very Shakespearean.

BALLOON   The fabric of this sleeve is full and balloon-shaped over the upper arm, then narrowed from the elbow to wrist.

POET   A sleeve that's gathered at the shoulder and very full from shoulder to cuff.

LONG/ILLUSION   Long sleeves—from shoulder to wrist—on gowns aren't as prevalent as they used to be, but one popular option is the "illusion" sleeve, made of a totally sheer fabric, which will make you *feel* covered up, though you won't necessarily look it.

BELL   This sleeve style is narrow from the armhole to below the elbow, then wide at the wrist.

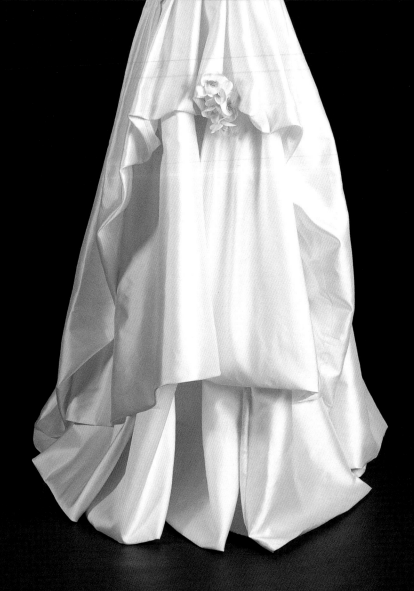

33 | 34                    | 35

# SKIRT

Whether full or flared, the skirt is where much of a gown's personality can be found: A few well-placed details can add length and volume, romance and depth, making the difference between a gown that's average and one that's out of this world. Some skirt details—strategically placed slits or pleats—can up a gown's sex appeal; others, such as delicate flounces, can make it more poetic. Techniques like folds or draping, as well as overskirts and overlays, can add visual interest, while shapes like the mermaid and trumpet are pure drama. Consider the bustle: Yards of fabric at the back of the skirt are gathered up and secured—a process known as "bustling"—with a few discreet buttons or hooks following the ceremony or the first dance. The end result? Swaths of fabric that add fullness and fun.

The length of your dress can dictate the formality of your wedding. Generally speaking, the longer the dress, the more formal the affair; floor-length is considered the most formal. Gowns that fall anywhere from mid-calf to the ankle are considered semiformal. And a gown that's knee length or shorter is said to be informal, though today the mini dress is considered a chic option for the unconventional sophisticate or second-time bride.

FIGURE 32  The side-swept pickups on this silk mikado ball gown add fullness and produce a modern asymmetrical effect.

FIGURE 33  A fishtail lends formality and an element of sophisticated surprise to the bottom of a satin peau de soie sheath.

FIGURE 34  A flurry of ruffles is a whimsical addition to a lightweight, airy silk organza sheath.

FIGURE 35  A bustle back adds dimension to this striped duchesse satin and organza gown, and sweeps the floor with a touch of tradition.

FIGURE 36  Two side "petals" bring fullness and formality to this slim-fitting satin sheath.

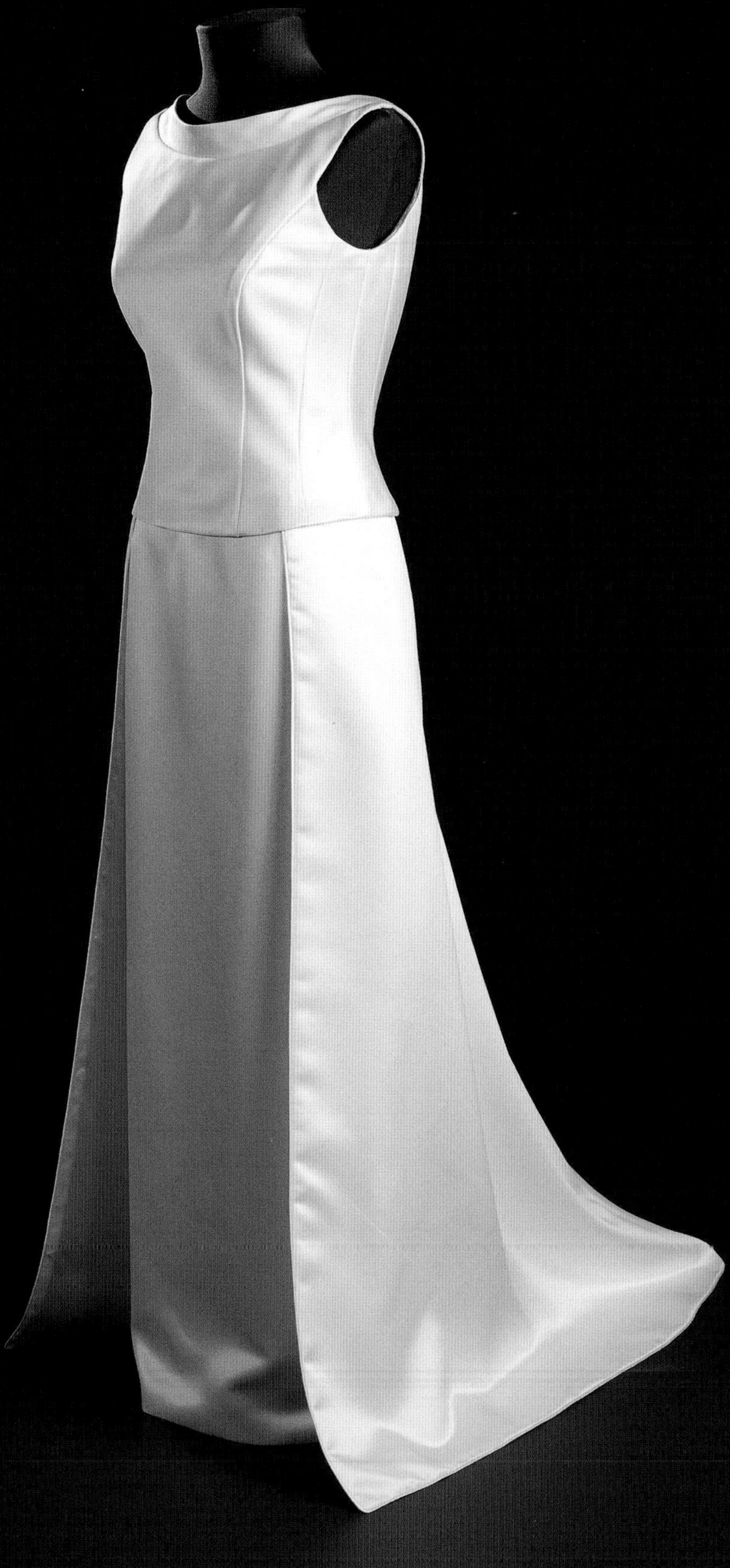

ACCORDION PLEATS     BOX PLEAT     BUSTLE     DRAPING     FLOUNCE

PETAL     STREAMERS     TAILS     TIERED

**ACCORDION PLEATS**   Close-together pleats that boast folds resembling the bellows of an accordion. The edges all face in one direction.

**BOX PLEAT**   Folds of fabric pressed on top to form a flat, box-shaped pleat; an inverted pleat is formed between each box pleat.

**BUSTLE**   Bunches of fabric (or the train) gathered at the back of a gown, secured with buttons or hooks.

**DRAPING**   Swaths of fabric pleated or gathered to a side or back seam of a skirt, adding fullness.

**FLOUNCE**   A wide ruffle around the bottom of a skirt.

**PETAL**   A type of overskirt that falls in rounded sections (similar to the petals of a flower) and usually reveals an underskirt of a different fabric.

**STREAMERS**   Strings or ties that trail down the back of the gown.

**TAILS**   Panels of the same or contrasting fabric, which trail behind the gown like a train.

**TIERED**   A skirt made of layers of various-length fabrics.

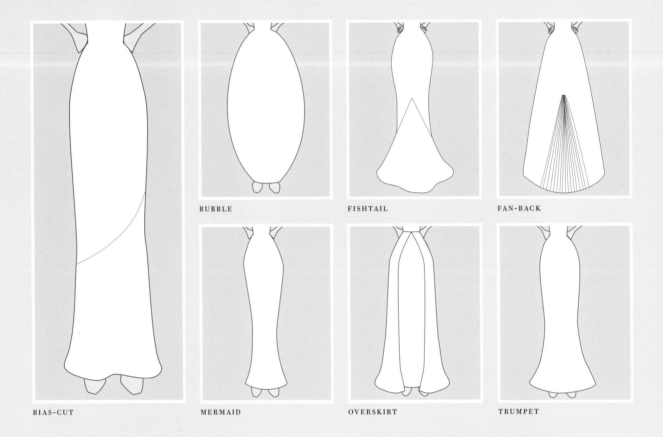

BIAS-CUT

BUBBLE

FISHTAIL

FAN-BACK

MERMAID

OVERSKIRT

TRUMPET

BIAS-CUT  Cut on the diagonal, or bias, of the fabric.

BUBBLE  A skirt gathered to a small waistline, then ballooned out and tapered in at the hem.

FISHTAIL  A skirt with an additional, stitched-on panel in the back, simulating a fishtail.

FAN-BACK  A skirt with accordion pleats in the back, extending from just below the waist or knees.

MERMAID  A slim, tapered, curve-hugging skirt that follows the line of the hips and thighs and flares out below the knee.

OVERSKIRT  A second skirt that lies over the main skirt, covering it partially without coming together in the front.

TRUMPET  A straight-lined skirt that flares toward the hem, like the mouth of a trumpet.

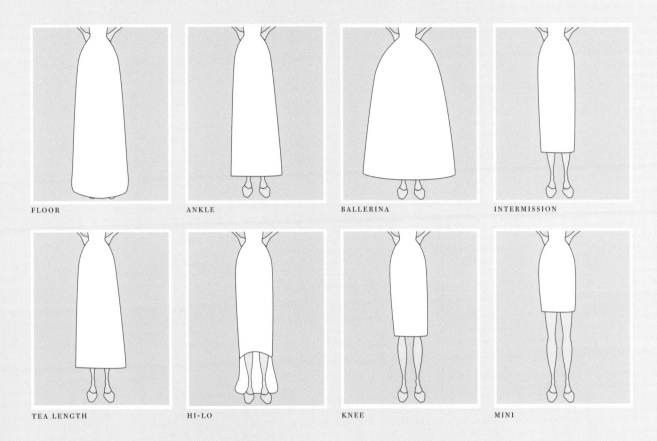

FLOOR    ANKLE    BALLERINA    INTERMISSION

TEA LENGTH    HI-LO    KNEE    MINI

**FLOOR** The hem on this gown brushes the floor on all sides. A wonderful formal look that works well on both straight and full gown styles.

**ANKLE** The ankle-length gown is hemmed right at the ankles. A nice semiformal option that can be either full or formfitting.

**BALLERINA** Like the name implies, the ballerina features a full skirt (think tutu) that reaches to just above the ankles. Very fun and flirty—great for an outdoor wedding.

**INTERMISSION** This hem falls anywhere between the knee and the ankle. Perfect for a semiformal or more casual affair.

**TEA LENGTH** A gown hemmed to a few inches below the knee. Conservative, but with a modern twist.

**HI-LO** A variation of the intermission, the hi-lo features an intermission hem on the front, and a floor-length (or longer) hem in the back. A popular look for bridesmaids.

**KNEE** Another great look for maids or for a casual bride, this style of skirt ends just below the knee.

**MINI** For the super-sassy bride—a skirt that ends mid-thigh.

37 | 38

39 | 40

# TRAIN

No matter what shape your dress is, a train can completely transform your look, allowing you to change the feel of your outfit from ceremony to reception. The train is simply the elongated back portion of the gown that lies on the floor and trails behind the bride, the added weight demanding a tall and majestic stance. Trains date from the Middle Ages, when the length worn at court indicated a person's social rank: The wealthier you were, the more fabric you could afford. Today, gowns with long chapel and cathedral trains are considered the most formal, lending themselves to bustling following the ceremony. Watteau trains (which spill from the shoulder) and court trains (which start from the waist) are less formal. The sweep gently puddles about a foot behind the wearer, and the detachable train—which can be any length and either a flat panel or gathers of fabric—is generally attached to the gown at the waist via buttons or hooks, then later removed for a less imposing look.

FIGURE 37 The sweep train on this silk charmeuse and organza A-line gently puddles about a foot behind the wearer.

FIGURE 38 The box pleats on the back of this platinum organza ball gown drape in luxurious folds to a dramatic chapel train.

FIGURE 39 A train of cascading ruffles on the back of this strapless silk satin sheath adds body and dimension, as well as an element of fun and flirtation.

FIGURE 40 This silk satin sheath features a smooth, wide court train for added formality, though it's still less formal than a gown with a chapel or cathedral version.

FIGURE 41 The lightweight organza train on this silk ball gown offers chapel length without the added weight of a heavier fabric.

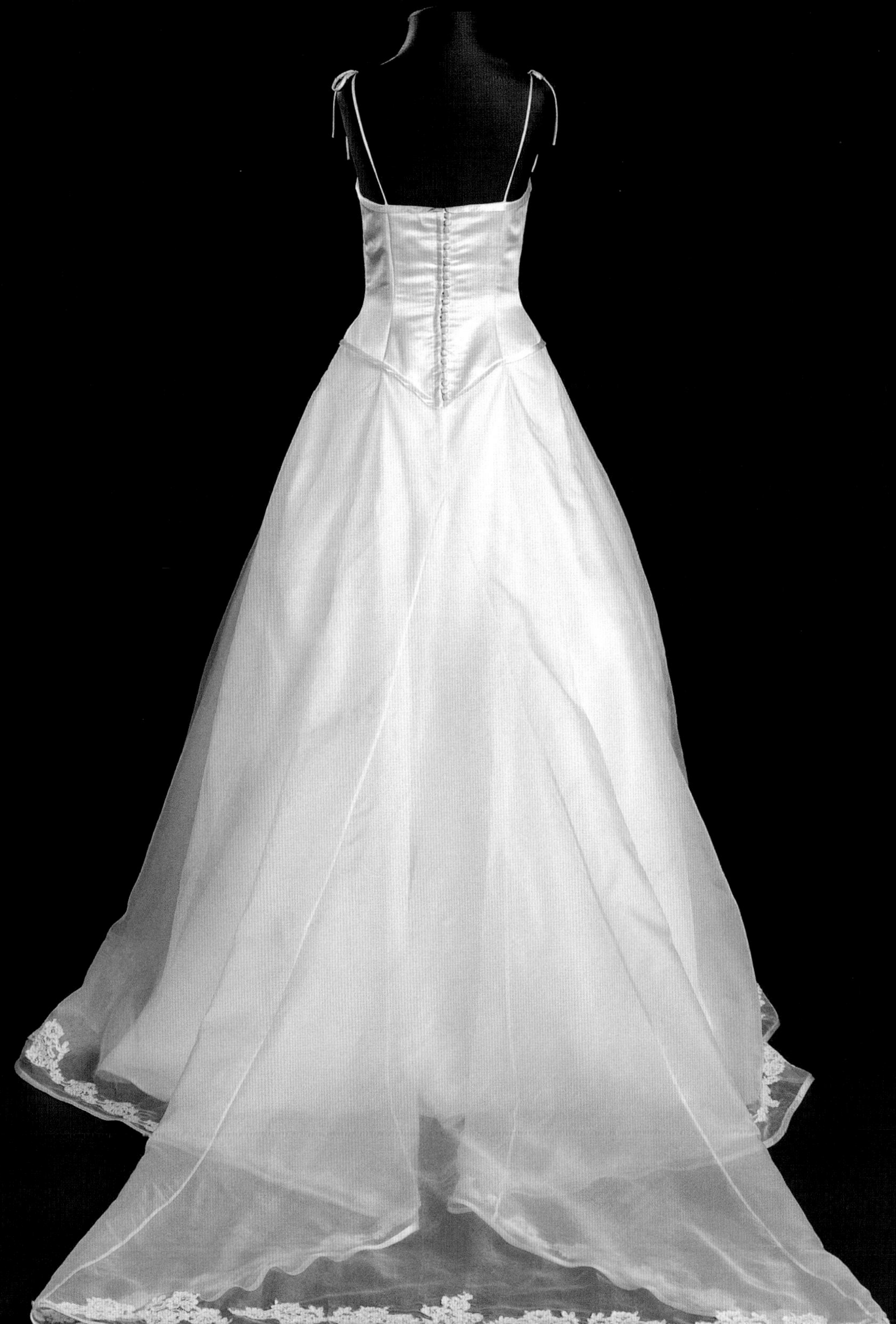

SWEEP

WATTEAU

COURT

CHAPEL

PANEL

CATHEDRAL

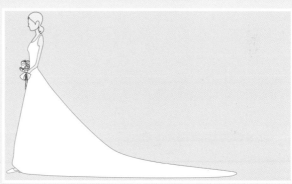

MONARCH

SWEEP  The shortest train, extending back 1 ½ feet or less from where the gown hits the floor. Also called *brush*.

WATTEAU  A train that attaches to the gown at the shoulders and falls loosely to the hem.

COURT  The same length as a sweep train, the court train extends directly from the waist.

CHAPEL  A very popular length, the chapel extends from 3 ½ to 4 ½ feet from the waist.

PANEL  A separate simple panel of fabric about a foot wide that acts as a train; can be court or chapel length and is often detachable.

CATHEDRAL  A very formal option, the Cathedral extends 6 ½ to 7 ½ feet from the waist.

MONARCH  Also know as *royal,* this version extends twelve feet or more from the waist. Managing such a huge amount of fabric often requires pages, young boys who hold up the train as you walk down the aisle.

# FABRIC

FIGURE 42   The skirt of this A-line gown gets its distinct shape and surface luster via silk mikado, a fabric woven with finely spun fibers.

FIGURE 43   This ball gown is smooth yet crisp, with a slight sheen, thanks to a rich combination of silk satin and taffeta.

FIGURE 44   More crisp and full but equally ethereal is this ball gown made of embroidered organza.

FIGURE 45   Layers and layers of gathered tulle netting give this ball gown its fullness and a weightless ballerina feel.

FIGURE 46   This airy ball gown is perfect for summer, as its silk gazar fabric is crisp and lightweight.

FIGURE 47   This A-line gown gets its floaty fullness from gathered silk chiffon.

Texture, drape, and season are all important factors in determining the best fabric for a wedding gown. The same style of dress can look and feel quite different in a different fabric, since each material is designed to produce a distinct effect. Some light-as-air knit fabrics cling to the body, while other more crisply woven varieties keep their structure and stand away. Some fabrics reflect light, some absorb it; some have a distinct shine, while others are matte.

44 | 45

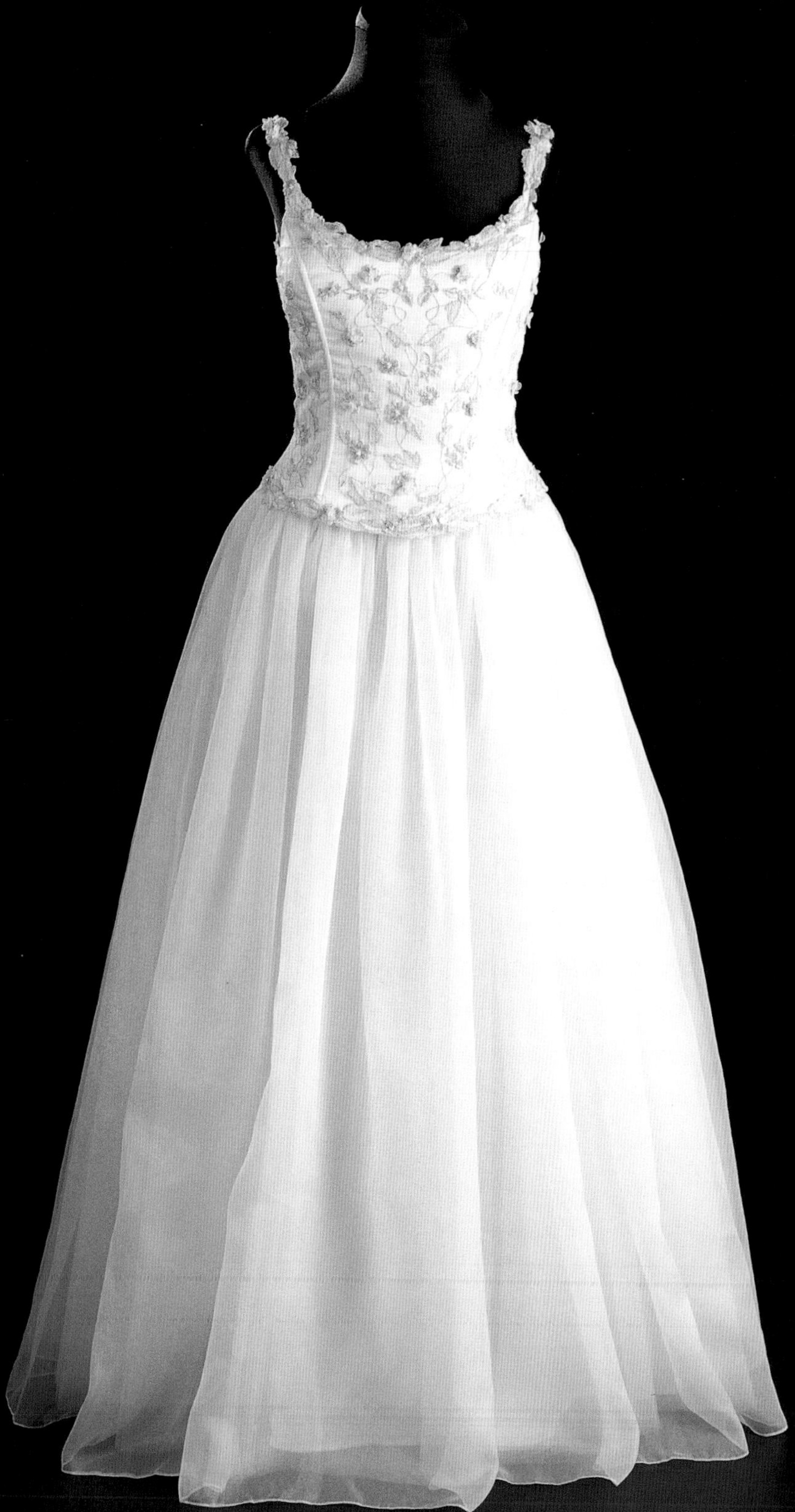

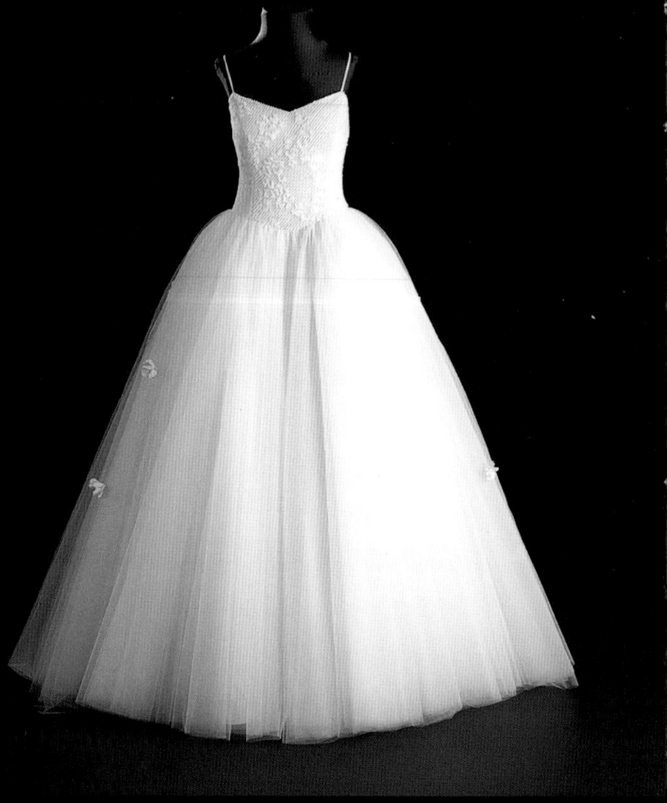

| 46

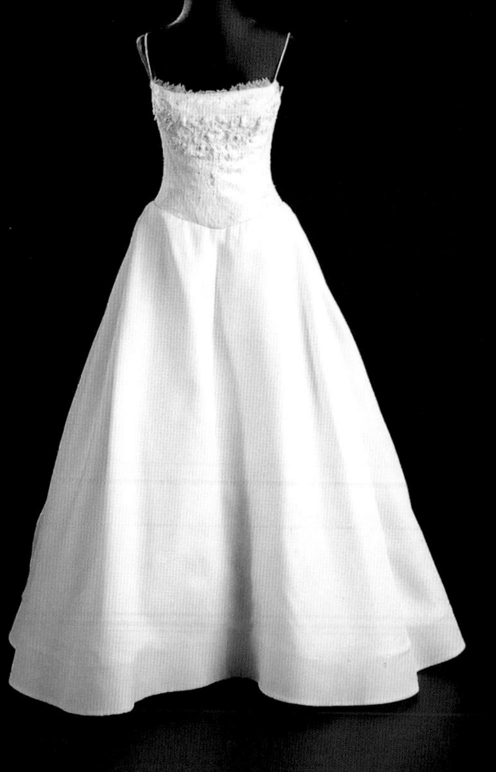

# FABRIC

Silk, a natural fiber and undoubtedly the fabric most often used for wedding dresses, is noted for its luster, resiliency, elasticity, and strength. Silk threads are woven to create satin (a dense fabric notable for its lustrous gloss), duchesse satin (a blend of silk and rayon that is lighter in weight and more affordable than pure silk satin), charmeuse (a lightweight satin with a more subdued luster), and shantung (a low-sheen textured fabric characterized by a nubby quality). Silk can also be knit into drapey, stretchy fabrics like jersey or crepe. Then there are gauzier woven silks, such as chiffon, tulle, and organza, all used for skirts in multiple layers as they are transparent but lightweight.

# GLOSSARY OF FABRICS

| FABRIC | QUALITIES | FIBERS | WEIGHT | CLIMATE | USES |
|---|---|---|---|---|---|
| Batiste | Soft, fine-textured, transparent weave | Mercerized cotton, cotton blended with poly or silk | Light | Warm weather | Loosely fitted silhouettes |
| Brocade | Rich jacquard weave with raised designs, often in contrasting colors or metallic threads | Silk, or silk blends | Heavy | Traditionally fall and winter; now seasonless | Structured and tailored gowns or coats; very formal |
| Charmeuse | Smooth, semi-lustrous, soft weave; similar to satin but lighter in weight; beautiful drape | Silk or manmade fibers | Light | Seasonless | Silhouettes requiring drape and fluidity |
| Chiffon | Delicate, sheer, fluid, and drapey weave with a matte finish | Nylon, poly, silk, or rayon | Very light | Seasonless | Great for sleeves, layers, veils; overlays on opaque fabric |
| Crepe | Crinkled or grained in texture | Acetate, rayon, silk, or blends | Light | Seasonless | Informal flowing gowns |
| Damask | Jacquard fabric with floral or geometric designs woven in; pattern is distinct from ground by contrasting luster | Acetate, cotton, linen, rayon, silk, wool, or manmade blends | A heavier look, like brocade, though fabric is lighter in weight | Fall, winter, spring | Structured and tailored gowns |
| Duchesse satin (also known as silk-faced satin) | Smooth, glossy, very lustrous weave with a matte back | Silk or silk/rayon blend | Medium | Seasonless | Formal looks; beautiful for simple designs or with embellishments |
| Dupioni | Weave is similar to shantung but less refined, with coarser fibers and a slight sheen | Silk | Light to medium | Traditionally spring through fall, now seasonless | Silhouettes needing a light feel but crisp hand |
| Empress silk satin | Smooth; medium-to-high sheen | Silk | Medium | Seasonless | Plain and embellished styles |
| Eyelet | A woven fabric with cutout patterns that are stitched around their edges | Cotton, cotton blends, manmade fibers | Light | Warm weather | Informal, feminine looks |
| Faille | Structured, ribbed weave similar to grosgrain; subtle luster; tailors beautifully | Cotton, silk, wool, manmade fibers, or blends | Medium | Multiseason | Ideal for all types of cuts and silhouettes |
| Gabardine | Durable, with a diagonal weave | Cotton, silk, wool, manmade fibers, or blends | Medium to heavy | Seasonless | Tailored styles; a good support fabric for beading |
| Gazar | Airy, crisp, smooth, with a crisscross weave | Silk, or silk blends | Light | Summer heat | Trains, skirts, overlays |
| Georgette | Sheer and fine weave with a crepelike texture | Silk, poly, or manmade fibers | Light | Spring, summer, fall | Drapey, layered styles |

| FABRIC | QUALITIES | FIBERS | WEIGHT | CLIMATE | USES |
|---|---|---|---|---|---|
| Illusion | Very fine, sheer netting | Silk or nylon | Barely there | Seasonless | Sleeves, necklines, backs, inserts, veils |
| Jersey | Soft, elastic, stretchy knit | Rayon, silk, or wool | Light to medium | Seasonless | Slinky bias cuts |
| Mikado | Twill weave similar to taffeta; finely spun fibers create a surface luster | Silk or silk blends | Medium | Seasonless | Architectural cuts, sweeping skirts |
| Moire | Taffeta with subtle wavy design like a watermark | Acetate, cotton, rayon, or silk | Light to medium | Seasonless | Structured ball gowns, full skirts |
| Organdy | Stiff, transparent weave | Cotton | Very light | Traditionally spring and summer, now seasonless | Gowns requiring crisp shapes |
| Organza | Sheer-woven like chiffon, but crisper | Nylon, poly, rayon, or silk | Light | Traditionally spring and summer, now seasonless | Layering and overlays, veils, trains, full skirts |
| Peau de soie | Soft, satin-faced weave with a dull luster and fine rib | Silk or manmade fibers | Heavy | Seasonless, but can be warm to wear | Full and straight silhouettes |
| Pique | Waffle-textured, less-fluid weave | Cotton | Medium to heavy | Spring, summer | Informal, simple styles |
| Satin | Smooth weave with a high sheen on one side | Acetate, poly, silk, or manmade fibers | Medium to heavy | Seasonless | Any shape or style |
| Shantung | Similar to raw silk, with imperfections and a slubbed texture caused by thick and thin yarns; lighter weight and finer weave than dupioni | Cotton, rayon, or silk | Medium to heavy | Traditionally spring and summer, now seasonless | Adds texture to a gown |
| Swiss dot | Fine, sheer weave, with flocked or embroidered dots at regular intervals; dots may be in same or contrasting color | Cotton, cotton blends, or rayon | Light | Warm weather | Informal, feminine styles |
| Taffeta | Stiff, crisp weave, smooth with a crosswise rib; can have a slight sheen or dull finish | Silk or poly | Light | Seasonless | Structured ball gowns; full skirts |
| Tulle | Fine-mesh netting with a hexagonal pattern; machine made | Cotton, silk, or nylon | Very light | Seasonless | Skirts, veils; mixes well with other fabrics |
| Velvet | Plush and thick weave with a felted face and plain underside; can be embossed or patterned | Cotton, poly, rayon, silk, or manmade fibers | Heavy | Fall, winter | Softly structured silhouettes |

# LACE

Rich with history, lace covers while it reveals, adding a touch of centuries-gone-by grace to any bride. Lace making—which involves looping, braiding, and interlacing cotton, silk, nylon, and other types of thread to form a pattern—developed from methods of embroidery in the fifteenth century. By the Victorian era, few brides would marry without a touch of this intricate threadwork somewhere on their gown. Lace can be used as a subtle detail, like a trim or bodice overlay, or more dramatically from head to toe. Lace comes in hundreds of weaves and shades, from the bold decoration of Alençon and Guipure to the delicate finery of Chantilly.

FIGURE 48 A spaghetti-strap gown made entirely of soft French lace in a solid pattern on sheer net looks dramatic and romantic.

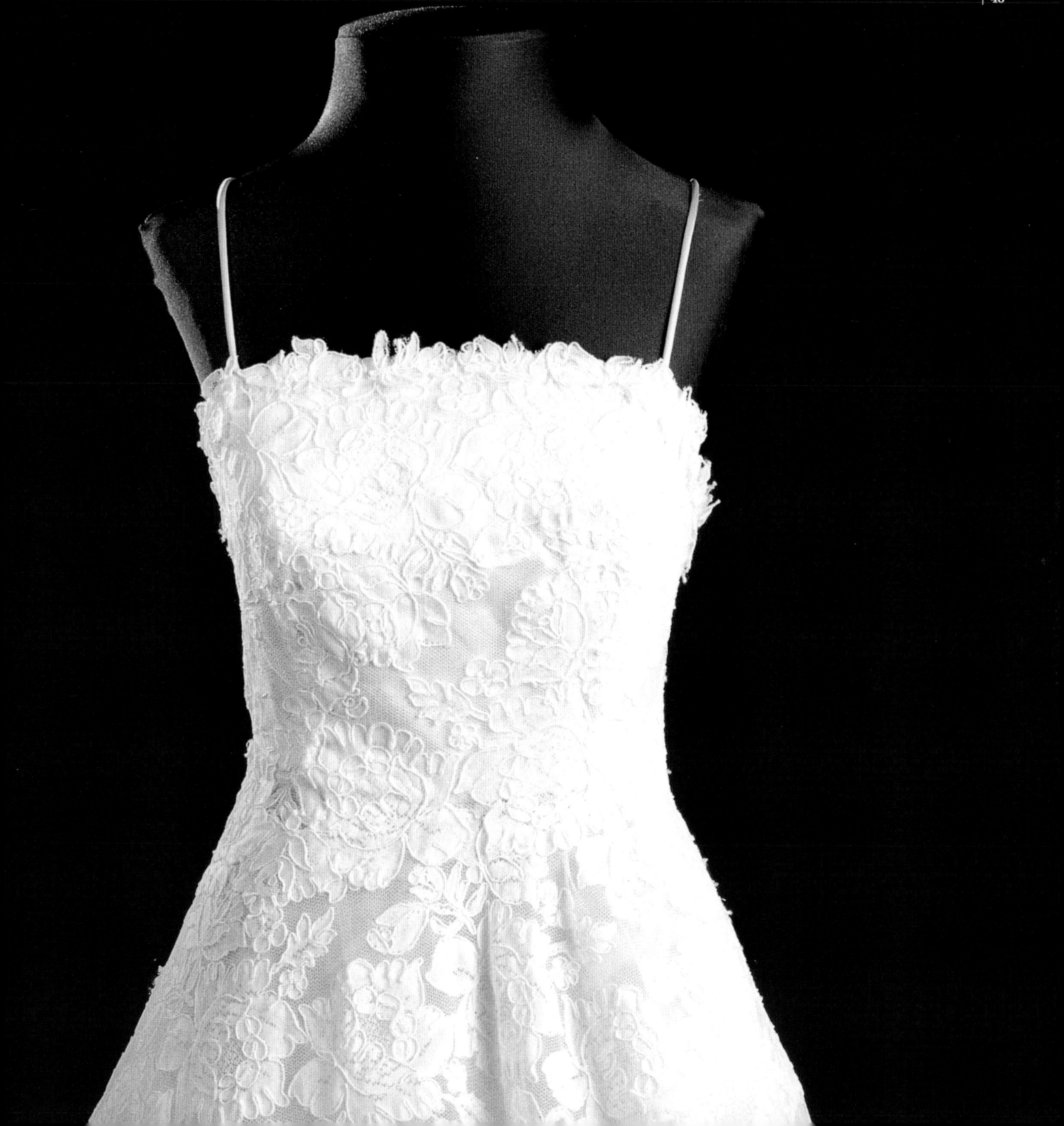

49 | 50

| 51

52 | 53

# LACE

FIGURE 49  A delicate whisper of Chantilly lace wrapped around the bodice gives this princess-line silk chiffon gown an ethereal effect, especially where the edges are left untrimmed.

FIGURE 50  The raised pattern of the heavy floral Venise lace on the bodice and hem of this Japanese matte satin ball gown adds texture and an organic element.

FIGURE 51  The golden fibers used in the lace on this silk organza ball gown lend a bejeweled look to the neckline, and a rich, majestic look to the skirt.

FIGURE 52  The branch motif of superfine French lace is a sophisticated addition on this short-sleeve sheath with matching sweep train.

FIGURE 53  All-over beaded lace adds richness to a halter-style silk satin bodice, while additional clusters of the same floral motif trim the hem to accent the English net skirt and sweep train.

## LACES

*Alençon: Needlepoint lace, with solid-relief motifs on sheer net, outlined with a heavier silky cording known as "gimp."*

*Chantilly: Features delicate floral, branch, and ribbon designs in heavy thread on a fine-mesh background; usually has scalloped edges where the edge threads ("eyelashes") are left uncut.*

*Guipure: A series of heavy, raised motifs connected by a few threads or on a coarse mesh background; offers a bold, sculpted look.*

*Honiton: A type of guipure lace with round, heavy floral and leaf motifs joined together over a mesh background.*

*Ribbon: Technically not a lace, but a pattern of ribbon sewn over a net background.*

*Schiffli: A lightweight machine-made lace, with an all-over delicate embroidered design.*

*Spanish: Lace with a distinctive flat design of roses on a net background; usually used for mantillas.*

*Venetian point: A heavy needlepoint lace with raised designs of floral sprays, foliage, or geometric patterns on an open background.*

# EMBELLISHMENT

Embellishments are like cake icing: They can add flavor, texture, and individuality to a simple, structured form. Through the centuries, brides have taken to adorning their wedding dresses to achieve a more striking appearance. Queen Victoria added fresh orange blossoms to her otherwise pure ensemble back in 1840, and throughout the eighteenth and nineteenth centuries it was widely believed that the more elaborately trimmed a woman's gown, the wealthier she was.

Today, it's the artistry and the visual effect of the embellishment that count. Elaborate beading and embroideries are used to add richness and texture to plain fabric. Small iridescent sequins are sewn on to add light and to give dresses a decorative "twinkle." And layers of fringe, cascades of crystals, and colorful beading—the "jewelry" of a gown—are all favored flourishes for adding the illusion of movement. Unique embellishments such as floral appliqués, feathers, or fur are fanciful additions that can take a gown from average to outrageous.

FIGURE 54 All-over flower-bud appliqués decorate this A-line silk organza gown.

FIGURE 55 A single floral appliqué on the back of a silk satin and floral-printed chiffon sheath punctuates the gown's feminine style and ups the romance factor.

FIGURE 56 Cascading crystals and pearls on the bodice of a silk ball gown add flowing glimmer.

54 | 55

| 56

57 | 58

| 59

| 60

# EMBELLISHMENT

FIGURE 57 The addition of a garland of leaf appliqués creates an asymmetrical effect on the skirt of this strapless gown.

FIGURE 58 Scattered clusters of beads provide understated sparkle and texture on the bodice of an A-line gown of English netting.

FIGURE 59 Colorful pink and moss floral embroidery animates a classic strapless sheath.

FIGURE 60 Tumbling swirls of embroidery on an asymmetrical princess-line gown of silk organza and duchesse satin lend texture and rhythm.

## EMBELLISHMENTS

*Appliqués: Fabric elements like flowers, ribbons, or cutouts stitched or embroidered onto a gown; sometimes raised.*

*Baroque pearls: Natural or simulated pearls of an irregular shape, often blue-gray or off-white.*

*Beading: Pieces of glass, crystal, gems, or other material sewn onto lace or fabric.*

*Border trim: Braided, ribboned, ruffled, or scalloped edging that provides a decorative effect.*

*Bows: Used in various lengths and sizes, from one giant butterfly bow to a tiny shoestring tie.*

*Bugle beads: Long, tubular glass beads, often black, white, or silver.*

*Crystals: Faceted and polished beads that reflect light.*

*Edging: A narrow decorative border of lace, embroidery, braid, or ribbon used for trim.*

# EMBELLISHMENT

FIGURE 61   A silk organza sheath gets added brilliance and depth from an extensive all-over pattern of sequins and seed beads.

FIGURE 62   The vertical beading on this Empire-waist tulle gown is designed to add motion and fluidity, plus lots of sparkle.

FIGURE 63   The vertical crystal beading on this silk chiffon A-line is graphic, yet airy, thanks to a willowy pattern that tapers off at each end.

FIGURE 64   Thick, twisting embroideries add motion, liveliness, and an organic quality to a princess-line silk gown.

FIGURE 65   The beads and embroidery tumbling down this silk tulle sheath produce a modern, flowing, asymmetrical effect.

*Embroidery: Fancy needlework patterns of various fine threads done by hand or machine.*

*Fringe: Ornamental trim consisting of loose strands of thread or beads fastened to a band.*

*Gems: Faux sparkling jewels such as rhinestones; often glued or sewn onto net or tulle.*

*Laser cut: Clean-edged intricate patterns cut into fabric via a laser.*

*Quilting: A sandwich of two layers of fabric and batting, which is then stitched in a pattern; offers subtle surface interest.*

*Seed pearls: Tiny genuine or simulated pearls used to adorn gowns, headpieces, and shoes.*

*Sequins: Tiny shiny, iridescent plastic disks sewn into place on a gown to add twinkle.*

*Paillettes: Larger versions of sequins, these shiny or matte plastic disks with a hole off-center at one end are sewn onto the gown to provide movement.*

61 | 62

| 63

64 | 65

# COLOR

Few traditions are as synonymous with Western weddings as wearing a white gown. However, as formal etiquette loses its hold and brides become more daring, the white dress has increasing competition. In recent seasons, bridal designers have shown assorted shades and hues for wedding wear, ranging from metallic platinum and gold to soft rose and lavender to pale blue. And more and more gowns are being designed with color in the details: everything from azure crystal beads to pink bands of satin. Even inside the world of white there is lots of variation, from warmer whites and ivories to crisp cold white, to blush, cocoa, and butterscotch. The white flattering to most skin tones is natural white, a shade softer than stark white (the whitest white) and found only in natural fibers like silk. Ivory, a creamy, warmer white with yellow undertones, is great for brides with fairer skin; and champagne, a white with pink undertones, is stunning on those with dark complexions.

FIGURE 66 This stark white ball gown of matte satin and tulle is the brightest, crispest white, and is beautiful on darker skin tones.

FIGURE 67 An extremely popular option in recent years, ivory looks beautiful on fair skin and adds richness to this silk shantung ball gown.

FIGURE 68 The natural white of this Italian silk mikado gown is a shade warmer than stark white, and is generally flattering to most skin tones.

FIGURE 69 The creaminess of this butterscotch satin organza ball gown is wonderful for medium skin with pink undertones.

FIGURE 70 Silverblue on a silk satin ball gown is a lustrous, elegant option for the unconventional bride.

FIGURE 71 The blush hue of this silk taffeta and tulle ball gown is a soft color good for most skin tones.

*Married in White, you have chosen all right,*
*Married in Gray, you will go far away,*
*Married in Black, you will wish yourself back,*
*Married in Red, you will wish yourself dead,*
*Married in Green, ashamed to be seen,*
*Married in Blue, he will always be true,*
*Married in Pearl, you will live in a whirl,*
*Married in Yellow, ashamed of your fellow,*
*Married in Brown, you will live out of town,*
*Married in Pink, your spirit will sink.*

—Old English rhyme

If you were to put stock in this popular old rhyme, there would be few acceptable colors in which a "sane" bride could wed, white being the obvious choice. Throughout many eras and in many countries and cultures, white came to be a sign of newness and purity, making it an ideal color in which to clothe a virgin bride for her wedding.

These days, white no longer holds such stringent symbolism; everyone—second-time brides included—is welcome to wear it. And while white has become a primary wedding color all over the globe, other colors take precedence in certain cultural circles.

# COLOR BY CULTURE

### AFRICA

Brides in some regions don *bubah:* brightly colored skirts, jackets, and head wraps. Others wear the cloth that represents their village in its color and pattern.

### CHINA

The traditional wedding dress is red, the Chinese color of joy and love, and is elaborately embroidered. Depending on the region, the dress may be a one-piece style similar to the *cheung sam* or a long jacket and skirt combination known as the *hung kwa.*

### INDIA

Bridal saris are generally made of silk embroidered with gold thread. Depending on the region, the color of silk may be red or white with a red border, or even a combination of yellow, green, and white.

### JAPAN

A white kimono lined in red is the garb of choice for Japanese brides, who may later change into an ornate colored robe, or *iro-uchikake,* in silver, gold, red, and white.

### KOREA

Brides first wear the green *wonsam,* and then change into the *hwarrot,* or flower robe. Both are liberally embroidered with flowers and butterflies and bands of symbolic color: red for heaven, indigo for earth, and yellow for humanity.

### SPAIN

Traditionally, Spanish Roman Catholic brides wear both a gown and lacey mantilla veil in black, as a symbolic promise of devotion to their husbands until death.

# DRESS PORTRAITS

Every gown—no matter what its size or shape—is a dynamic combination of elements working together to enhance and flatter the wearer's figure and to create a uniquely balanced vision. For instance, the sex appeal of a sheath can be softened with the addition of flirty floral embroideries, or high-lighted with a halter neckline and a sexy slit skirt. A big tulle ball gown can celebrate its princess appeal with lots of beading and a Basque waistline, or it can look more modern with box pleats and a simple strapless bodice.

Behold the design elements at work in each of the following six dress portraits:

PORTRAIT 1

## SOMETHING BLUE

The peacock-blue floral embroidery on this A-line gown is flirty and fun, and the sheer layers of French organdy add to its feminine appeal. An edge of sophistication creeps in as well, courtesy of the sweep train, square neckline, and sexy satin straps.

SILHOUETTE  A-line

FABRIC  French organdy

NECKLINE  Square

WAISTLINE  Natural

LENGTH  Floor

EMBELLISHMENT  Embroidery

DESIGNER  Robert Legere

PORTRAIT

# 2

# PURE & SIMPLE

A number of independent elements come together to create this well-proportioned spare and sophisticated look, which is traditional without being conventional. The deep-V dip of the neckline and the pleated Empire waist closely follow the lines of the body to produce a "molded" effect, while the softness of the organza skirt and chapel-length train blend to create a beautifully balanced gown.

SILHOUETTE  A-line

FABRIC  Silk shantung and organza

NECKLINE  V-neck

WAISTLINE  Empire

TRAIN  Chapel

DESIGNER  Carolina Herrera

# 3

PORTRAIT

# BOLD & BEAUTIFUL

This romantic silk tulle ball gown is designed for a majestic entrance, with its gold Alençon lace-covered bodice and sleeves, and a full tulle skirt finished with a scalloped hem. Generous amounts of boning help shape the Basque-waisted bodice, which is highlighted with metallic piping, a scoop neckline, and a regal lace-up back.

SILHOUETTE  Ball gown

FABRIC  Silk tulle

NECKLINE  Scoop

BODICE DETAIL  Boning

SLEEVES  Long and sheer

LENGTH  Floor

EMBELLISHMENT  Piping and lace

DESIGNER  Max Chaoul

# 4

# MIDAS TOUCH

This stunning duchesse silk satin gown gets its Elizabethan look and feel from an Empire waistline and cap sleeves. The A-line design is slimming, and the rich fabric and shimmery splashes of gold and platinum embroidery add a royal feeling.

SILHOUETTE  A-line

FABRIC  Silk duchesse satin

NECKLINE  Square

WAISTLINE  Empire

SLEEVES  Cap

EMBELLISHMENT  Embroidery

TRAIN  Sweep

DESIGNER  Melissa Sweet

PORTRAIT

# 5

## SLEEK & STRAPLESS

This gown's design allows the bride embellishment with a sleek look. The richly embroidered strapless bodice and slim A-line skirt give the ensemble a three-dimensional feel with a decidedly modern edge, while the flip side reveals a more traditional look: a row of covered buttons that leads to a full, pleated chapel-length train.

SILHOUETTE  A-line

FABRIC  Silk peau de soie

EMBELLISHMENT  Embroidery

COLOR  Ivory

TRAIN  Chapel

NECKLINE  Strapless

DESIGNER  Ines di Santo

PORTRAIT

6

# TO HAVE & TO HALTER

This gown is all about architecture and the way it highlights the lines of the wearer's body. The halter neckline is clean and elegant, cut to reveal strong shoulders and back, while the tightly fitted bodice and dropped waistline emphasize the midriff. Likewise, the skirt is cut so there's no bulkiness at the front, yet the two deep inverted front pleats add plenty of dimension, giving the illusion of added fullness and formality.

SILHOUETTE  Ball gown

FABRIC  Silk satin peau de soie

NECKLINE  Halter

WAISTLINE  Dropped

SKIRT DETAIL  Inverted pleats

TRAIN  Chapel

DESIGNER  Alfred Sung

# 3 | SHOPPING

**The hunt** for your wedding gown is exciting, emotional, and—we'll admit it—at times exasperating. You are presented with a world of options, and the pressure to find The Perfect Gown for one of the most important days of your life can be great. So how do you go about doing it? Think about what kind of a shopper you are: Do you generally have a pretty good idea of what you're looking for, or do you require a little assistance? Do you prefer to go it alone, or do you rely on a chorus of opinions? Do you crave the thrill of finding a "good deal," or do you savor the royal treatment of an exclusive boutique? All of these factors will come into play in your hunt. As for when to start, it's never too soon. We recommend starting the search for your gown anywhere from nine to twelve months before your wedding. In this chapter, we'll prep you on identifying your own bridal style and offer solutions for what types of gowns are best suited to your body type before you get out there and pound the pavement.

# FINDING YOURSELF

Dream a little, and get in touch with your inner bride. Close your eyes and envision yourself walking down the aisle. What do you see? Are you wearing a full ball gown with your hair in romantic ringlets? Or are you outfitted in an ethereal, flowing dress, with your hair loose and sprinkled with flowers? Should you go with a traditional look? A modern one? Or are you more of a bohemian?

Assess the clothes already in your closet. Which pieces do you love? Why? Which ones make you feel a certain way (beautiful, sexy, comfortable) or help you to assume a particular persona? These are some of the same things you'll be looking for in your gown. Then write down six adjectives that best describe how you want to look and feel on your wedding day: *summery, traditional, princesslike, sexy, sophisticated, over-the-top* are just a few suggestions. The image you conjure—royal queen or garden goddess—goes beyond your attire to drive the overall mood and feel of your wedding.

There are ways to effectively incorporate your personal sense of style into almost any ensemble for almost any ceremony, no matter what the situation. It's all in the details. If you're a country bride, why not have a ruffled skirt and lots of bows? If you're Scottish, add tartan trim to your gown. Are you an athlete? Change into your favorite running shoes for the reception, or Birkenstocks if you're the outdoorsy type. Even if you decide to go the straight up, by-the-book traditional route, you're still communicating your own personal sense of style.

# BRIDE TYPES

When you get right down to it, we're all characters with distinct traits, some of which are derived from clothes we like to wear, public people whom we admire, stories we read, movies we watch, activities we participate in, and even the moods we have. Coming to terms with this personality is a major step in identifying your bridal style. Who are you?

### THE PRINCESS

Idyllic? Sentimental? Knew your prince would come (some day)? Behold the princess bride—you're as girly as it gets. Ball gowns. Basque waists. Tons of tulle. Maybe even a corset. Embellishment is essential for you, so look for sparkly crystal beading and pearl drops. Heirloom-to-be additions: a tiara (natch), a bejewelled purse, and a dangling-little-something of the diamond variety.

### THE TRADITIONALIST

Audrey Hepburn. Grace Kelly. Jackie O. With these members of the classic style hall of fame as your guardian angels, the traditionalist bride is in good company. Your timeless look starts with a simple neckline (think jewel or bateau) and a skirt with straight lines flowing from a natural waist to a chapel train. Also on your checklist: your mother's pearls, a conservative clutch, proper pumps, and a lifetime of composure.

### THE SOPHISTICATE

You're a chic realist. Bustling city streets, museums, and European adventures are more your thing than dreamy ever-afters. So when it comes to your wedding, you want to look worldly and polished, not like a traditional blushing bride. Your look: a gown that's long, lean, and elegant; hair that's swept up high; jewels that sparkle from a mile away. The effect: undeniably thoroughbred.

### THE ROMANTIC

Poetry and sweet nothings send your head spinning? Secretly obsessed with your wedding day since age six? You're a romantic at heart, and *pretty* is your operative word. On your day, you'll clothe yourself in a gown with the most intricate embroidery or layer upon layer of the loveliest lace, and your hair will frame your face in wavy tendrils.

### THE DRAMATIST

Big, bold, over the top. You're a theatrical diva inspired by Marie Antoinette and the grande dames of the stage, with majesty and magic as your goals. Your wedding is an opportunity to costume yourself in finery fit for an empress, from poufy sleeves and a lavishly decorated bodice to a skirt out to *there* with layers of crinoline.

### THE BOHEMIAN

Fancy yourself a bit of a wild child? See yourself as an angel on earth? Your gown: breezy and simple, maybe even fairylike and ethereal. Your accessories: fuss-free flowers, and lots of them. Your makeup message: inner peace and tranquility. After all, nothing is more important than a day of free-flowing love and good karma.

### THE STARLET

Want to go glam on your wedding day? Your look is the perfect mix of charismatic style and screen-star sex appeal. A body-skimming bias cut is your dress of dreams. Décolletage is a given, and a low-cut back a bonus. You carry a wrap and yearn to drip with decadent jewels. The finishing touch? Incredibly kissable lips.

### THE VIXEN

You smolder. You sizzle. When you walk down the aisle, heads will turn. *Barely there* are two of your favorite words, and the more skin you show, the better. Your wedding is no time to be demure—being a sexy bride is your goal and you've got sex appeal in spades. Your mane of hair flows free, and your accessories of choice are pricey mile-high stilettos to show off your toes. Meow!

### THE MINIMALIST

Far from plain, you are thoroughly modern. "Less is more" is your mantra: No bows, beads, or embroidery for you. It's all about the architecture, and you prefer to keep it simple with one strategically placed detail, such as an asymmetrical peak or unique fold to the fabric. You'll carry a single favorite flower and wear a wedding band of pure platinum.

### THE FASHIONISTA

Do you possess an in-the-know instinct? Have a flair for what's hot? You're up to the minute, and your time is now. To you, a wedding is just another day to strut your fashion stuff. Whether you opt for the latest trend on the scene or outlandish one-of-a-kind ornaments, your choices will leave admirers gasping with awe.

# TAKING STOCK

To make your in-store adventure even more comfortable, take stock of your gown reality before you hit the stores. In other words, decide which of the following factors—the formality of your affair, the season, your budget, your religion, and ultimately, your body type—have the most influence on your decision, then look for gowns that fit the bill. Think of it as the most extraordinary recipe: The ingredients you set aside here are what will determine the overall "flavor" of the dress you'll eventually wear down the aisle.

FORMALITY While every bride should feel free to choose the wedding style of her dreams, her attire should also reflect the time and place of the nuptials. A formal candlelit ceremony is not the time for a bride to be sporting a short sundress. Nor is an afternoon garden party the place to break out the cathedral-length train. If your wedding is outdoors in a quixotic locale, choose an equally romantic look for your ceremony—say, a flirty ankle-length dress with embroidered leaves and vines. Likewise, if your party is planned in a proper reception hall, consider more classic to-be-wed ensembles that mimic the mood, or celebrate your inner cool-cat-ness with a sleek asymmetrical gown. Go for drama in a theatrical setting with an over-the-top gown. And embrace the setting at a beach wedding with a two-piece dress, a pair of sheer flowing pants, or a daring white bikini.

BUDGET You'll need to set a budget before you hit the stores. Dress prices range widely, from $750 to $15,000. The average gown is around $2,000. Dresses in the lower price ranges are typically made in assembly-line fashion, while couture dresses are more handcrafted. Deciding how much money you're willing to shell out for your gown is step number one: 10 percent of your total wedding budget is usually a good guideline, though if you're willing to cut back on other areas of your planning process in order to spring for the dress of your dreams, more power to you! Just don't forget to factor in your veil and headpiece (which can run from $100 to over $500), as well as accessories such as shoes, jewelry, lingerie, and a purse, which can run anywhere from $50 to $500 (and up!) per item.

## PRICE BREAKDOWN

Based on your budget, you may spend $800 or $8,000 on your gown. Though you might find gowns in both of these ranges that look surprisingly similar, there are differences in construction and quality of materials. And while price does not necessarily make one gown better than another (and rest assured, you'll look gorgeous in whatever gown you choose), it helps to understand what factors might contribute to the cost of a gown.

FABRIC

Cost Contributor: Natural silk

Cost Cutter: Manmade fabric or silk blend

CUT

Cost Contributor: A refined pattern for the best fit

Cost Cutter: A mass-produced pattern that accommodates the most body types

BEADING

Cost Contributor: Crystal beads and genuine pearls handsewn to fabric

Cost Cutter: Glass beads and faux pearls glued to fabric

EMBROIDERY

Cost Contributor: Hours of hand stitching

Cost Cutter: Machine stitching

DESIGNER

Cost Contributor: Well known or exclusive

Cost Cutter: Lesser known

SEASON  The weather will also play a role in what you wear. How? Certain dress fabrics lend themselves better to certain times of year and/or climates. Generally speaking, silk satin or mikado works well in all types of weather, while brocades and velvets work better in cold climates, chiffons and linens in warmer ones. (See Glossary of Fabrics, pages 74–75).

RELIGION  When it comes to religious considerations, the best thing to do is check with your ceremony officiant to find out if he/she has any guidelines or specific restrictions concerning bridal attire. Depending on your religion and/or ethnic background, your officiant may insist that your head, legs, or shoulders be covered: Orthodox Jewish brides, for example, need to cover all three and don a blusher, while Mormon brides traditionally wear a gown with a high neck and long sleeves. If you wait until the last minute (that is, the day of the wedding) to reveal your plans, don't be surprised if the officiant refuses to start the ceremony until you cover up.

BODY TYPE  Choosing a dress that flatters your figure is the decision that will make you most comfortable on your big day, so it's important that you assess your body type before you start shopping. Learn which shapes and styles best suit your figure, and you'll have an easier time finding the gown that makes you feel the most comfortable and confident. See the following pages for some general guidelines.

## BROAD

*You're built like a swimmer,*
*with wide-set shoulders.*

DRESS DOS: Expose your beautiful
shoulders with a halter, or go for drama in
a gown with long sleeves worn off the
shoulder. Select a dress with a narrow
bodice that offsets your shoulders and
creates an hourglass shape.

DRESS DON'TS: Trying to conceal your
shoulders is not recommended, as it
sometimes produces the opposite effect.

## FULL-FIGURED

*Voluptuous, with a well-endowed*
*bust and curvy hips.*

DRESS DOS: Try ball gowns with a Basque
waist, which has a slimming effect. A high-
waisted A-line dress with a low neckline also
flatters curves.

DRESS DON'TS: A slim sheath or slinky
bias cut will cling and may accent any extra
inches; also avoid spaghetti straps.

## BUSTY

*Petite, plus, or average size,*
*you've got a full bust.*

DRESS DOS: Accentuate the positive with
an uplifting foundation garment and an
off-the-shoulder bodice. Or, curtail your
curves with a one-piece minimizer worn
under a gown that boasts a fitted bodice to
emphasize your waist, a jewel neck, and cap
sleeves. Balance your top with a full skirt.

DRESS DON'TS: Be careful not to overdo
the bareness—you want the focus to be on
your face. And don't forget to move around
in your gown during fittings to make sure
everything stays in place.

# BODY TYPES

## PEAR-SHAPED

*Though small on top, you round off*
*toward the bottom.*

DRESS DOS: A Basque waist or strapless
ball gown will cover your bottom half
and focus on your better half; an off-the-
shoulder neckline will make your top look
more in proportion to your bottom.

DRESS DON'TS: A sheath can be
unflattering, and a V-neck will draw the
eyes downward, where you don't want
them to go.

## BOXY

*Short or tall, you have a boyish waistline.*

DRESS DOS: Empire-waisted gowns are
made with you in mind. And a ball gown
with a Basque waistline will give you the
nipped-in look you crave.

DRESS DON'TS: Steer clear of sheaths and
dropped waists, which will make you look
even more boxy.

## PETITE

*You're a teeny, tiny slip of a thing.*

DRESS DOS: The key word here is *elongation.* It's best to keep it simple. A columnlike sheath or A-line dress will work well: These shapes create a long interrupted line. Stick to open, sexier necklines—think strapless and off-the-shoulder styles, both of which work beautifully.

DRESS DON'TS: Almost all silhouettes will flatter your figure, though a big ball gown or a dress with lots of voluminous fabric may overwhelm (when you're small, a big, elaborate gown can sometimes look as if it's wearing you rather than the other way around).

## TALL

*Five-feet-ten or taller.*

DRESS DOS: Tall women look great in everything from sheaths (if you're also slim) to A-lines and full ball gowns. Accentuate your collarbone with a fitted bodice and open neckline. Then top your look with a long veil—you can carry it off.

DRESS DON'TS: Skip gowns that boast high necks and long sleeves, and steer clear of updos and headpieces that add too much extra height.

## BONY

*Short or tall, you're not a fleshy woman.*

DRESS DOS: A ball gown will make you look like a beautiful ballerina. It's a very feminine shape that will balance out your overall silhouette. Try one with a dramatic cutout back.

DRESS DON'TS: If you're concerned your collarbone is too bony, stay away from portrait, off-the-shoulder, or halter necklines. And if you're also flat chested, avoid a darted bodice made of stiff fabric.

## PREGNANT

*You've got a baby belly, anywhere from 4 to 9 months!*

DRESS DOS: Buying a gown while pregnant can be tricky, since you can't predict how big you'll be come wedding day. You can wait until the date gets closer and then buy a dress off the rack, or you can order something you'll grow into. In this respect, an Empire or A-line style is your best bet for its loose structure and relaxed silhouette. For the daring mom-to-be who wants to show off her condition, a soft clinging sheath in a stretchy fabric makes a proud statement.

DRESS DON'TS: Obviously avoid anything that's too constricting or uncomfortable, including tight bodices and ball gowns, which will only emphasize your expanding middle.

## ARM ISSUES

*You're self-conscious about your arms, whether they're heavy, jiggly, or too skinny.*

DRESS DOS: Choose long or three-quarter-length sleeves, or go for barely-there coverage with sexy sleeves made from sheer illusion fabric.

DRESS DON'TS: Steer clear of off-the-shoulder sleeves and cap-sleeve gowns, which highlight the upper arms.

NOTE: Even though certain styles work best on certain body types, don't let the "rules" narrow your search too much. It helps to try on all different kinds of dresses, then decide what shape and style you look and feel best in.

# WHERE TO SHOP

If you've ever walked past a bridal boutique and stopped to gaze at the gorgeous creations in the window, then you've already been touched by the inherent romance of the salon. As a necessary destination in any bride's wedding planning, the bridal salon is inextricably linked to the notion of two people joining in love, calling up such emotions as passion, hope, and joy. But unless you're working with a stylist or personal shopper, your actual in-store experience can be overwhelming, intimidating, and riddled with questions. What really happens inside salons? What's expected of you? And how far in advance of the wedding do you need to visit one?

The two words to keep in mind are *shop early*. Nine to twelve months before the wedding is ideal, since it's best to have about six months to spare for fittings. Why? Unless you buy a ready-to-wear dress or a sample gown, salon wedding dresses are custom-made (and all that exotic beading is likely handsewn). Then, once the dress arrives, it must be altered—usually several times—to fit you perfectly. That said, many salons can turn a dress around quickly. If you have less than six months, start shopping now and try to be flexible about your dress choice. One tip: Go simple. As a rule, the less complicated the dress, the less time it takes to make and fit.

If you have lots of time, you can hit every salon, shop till you drop, and agonize over your gown decision. Try to avoid weekends and evenings, though, if you can swing it, as bridal salons are insanely busy at these times. If you can take time off during the week to shop, you'll get more of the salesperson's time and attention.

WHAT'S IN STORE Bridal salons are known for their personal service, tranquil yet formal setting, and assembly of custom-made designer wedding gowns. Each spring and fall, wedding gown designers gather in New York, Chicago, Las Vegas, and Dallas for bridal markets, biannual fashion shows during which they present their new lines to bridal shop owners, so that they in turn can buy them and sell them to you.

## LOOKING ONLINE

Thanks to the growth of the Internet and wedding-specific Web sites like The Knot, it's now possible to research the perfect gown without leaving the house. The benefit of browsing this way (notice we didn't say "buying"—you'll still want to try on the real thing before making a purchase) is that, with the click of a mouse, you can check out thousands of gown styles and designers, and find out where they are available in your area. Heck, you can even print out door-to-door driving directions.

The Internet offers a time-saving method of looking for gowns that's hard to top: In no time, you can zero in on what you like and what you wouldn't even consider trying on. Try locating your favorite designer's Web site to gather info on where you can see his or her gowns at a location near you. Or check out The Knot (www.theknot.com/gowns), where you can browse thousands of gowns by whatever method you choose: designer, style, price range, and store location.

Unless you're planning to wear your mother's gown or have one made, the bridal salon is the best place to find your dream dress. You'll find boutique salons in upscale urban shopping districts, suburban downtown areas, strip malls, large malls, and even inside some of the larger department stores. Check local bridal magazines or the Internet to see what's available in your area. Word-of-mouth recommendations are also very helpful. Find out which shops have given excellent service to past brides, then call to make appointments.

Besides the day-to-day business of selling dresses, salons also hold special wedding-related events like trunk shows and sample sales. At a trunk show, a specific designer (or representative of a bridal manufacturer) brings his or her latest dress line for brides-to-be to try on during a special in-store gathering. The advantage? You get to see every dress in the line, not just the styles selected by the store. And you may even get the small thrill of chatting with the designer in person—or better yet, having him or her assess your look.

Since the gowns in bridal salons don't come cheap—expect to pay at least $1,000 and up to $10,000 for full service and a custom-ordered garment made by a top bridal designer—many brides covet the sample sale. Though there's lots of mystery and intrigue surrounding these events, basically a sample sale is just what it sounds like: the sale of the dresses that were used in the salon as try-on samples. Some stores have samples in an array of sizes, though the general sample sizes are 6, 8, and 10. Keep in mind that wedding dresses run small, so if your regular dress size is a 2, 4, or 6, you may be in luck. The dresses may not be super-clean, but if you get a great price, you can put some of your savings towards the cleaning bill.

# SHOPPING TIPS

On your first time out, try to limit your shopping spree to three or four different salons, since it's easy to forget which gowns you tried on where. Bring along a notebook to jot down notes regarding the gowns you like and the way you're being treated in each shop. Are the salespeople regarding you respectfully? Or are they acting haughty? This is where all the knowledge you've armed yourself with will come in handy. If you can speak expertly about dress silhouettes and styles, the salesperson will know she's dealing with an informed consumer.

ACCEPTING HELP When you get to the bridal salon, a specific salesperson will be assigned to you. You will work with this person every time you return to the store. A good salesperson will ask you what type of wedding you're having, how you envision yourself looking on your wedding day, and what kinds of dresses you're drawn to. She will also probably check you out and decide for herself what kinds of dresses will look good on you based on your body type. Then she'll bring you dresses to try on (most salons don't allow you to browse through the racks; they'll assign you a dressing room, ask you what you're looking for, then bring gowns to you). Your salesperson will likely want to dress you as well. Let her. Wedding gowns are often heavy, complicated, or fragile, and salespeople know how to get you in and out of them.

Take advantage of a salesperson's expertise. She works with brides every day; if anyone knows about dresses, she does. Try not to eliminate anything she brings you at first glance—even if you detest the way it looks on the hanger. Many a bride has ended up waltzing down the aisle in a gown the salesperson had to persuade her to try on. Feel free to bounce ideas off of her and consider her advice if you think it's given in good faith. But if anyone tries to talk you in or out of something, or makes you feel uncomfortable about your decisions, remember: A good salesperson will never pressure you to buy something you're unsure about.

Some questions to consider when calling
bridal salons to make appointments:

What size sample dresses are available for
you to try on?

Do they carry the designers you're
interested in?

Do they have gowns in your price range?

Will there be shoes and undergarments
for you to try on with the gowns?

If you like a gown the store doesn't carry,
will they order a sample for you to try on?
If so, are you then obligated to buy
the dress?

How long does it generally take for a
dress to come in once it's been ordered?
Can the order be rushed, if necessary?

Can you see a fabric sample from the
dress you're thinking of ordering (since
sample dresses can be discolored
from wear)?

Does the store carry headpieces and
other accessories?

Can you get a written alteration estimate
when you order your dress?

If your bridesmaids order their dresses
through this store, do you receive a discount?

WHO AND WHAT TO BRING When shopping for the first time, you'll probably want to bring along an extra set of eyes. Your mom, sister, honor attendant, bridesmaids, close friends, or relatives whom you trust top the who-gets-to-go list. But try to maintain crowd control: Limit the entourage to no more than three friends or family members at once. Otherwise, you'll feel overwhelmed (and so will your salesperson). There will be more than one shopping trip—trust us—so everyone can have a turn.

When you're trying on gowns, you'll want to get a sense of the way the entire package will look on you. This means bringing along some accessories. Most stores will have petticoats and shoes available to you while trying on dresses, but for the truest fit, it's best to bring your own. The short list: a strapless bra or bustier, panty hose, and a pair of shoes with a heel height that matches the one you plan to wear for your wedding (obviously, you don't need to have the exact pair yet). Pay close attention to how your underpinnings and hosiery interact with the gown; for example, if you plan to wear a bustier or control-top pantyhose, be mindful of their visual presence beneath sheer or unlined fabric or clingy silhouettes.

In addition to accessories, bring along some bottled water, as trying on gowns all day in a cramped dressing room can leave you dehydrated. Dried-fruit snacks and bananas are also good tag-alongs, as are pocket-size tissues for Mom, and a Polaroid camera. Though cameras are basically off limits while shopping—salons need to guard against brides taking a picture of the gown, then getting a dressmaker to copy it—once you've put a deposit down on *the one*, you'll want to remember what it looks like.

# DECISION TIME

You didn't get engaged on your first date, right? Likewise, you shouldn't buy the first dress you try on. Give yourself all the options and the time to think by shopping more—and elsewhere—before you buy.

You may even want to try shopping on your own at least once. It sounds like the exact opposite of what you'd expect wedding dress shopping to be like, right? But chances are, after you've gotten into the swing of things, you'll be the most focused on which dresses feel right when you're alone in the dressing room. Maybe you'll narrow down the choices on your own, then invite Mom and Sis to help pick the winner.

MAKING IT YOUR OWN  Even after you think you've found your gown, you'll still have some important decisions to make. One of the biggest misconceptions about bridal gowns is that they're only available in the sample form. The truth is, most gowns are offered in a variety of versions, so be sure to ask your salesperson about the different fabrics or sleeve lengths available in a particular silhouette. Most gowns can be ordered in alternative forms, so if you like the bodice of one and the skirt of another, ask to have them put together to make your dream dress (provided, of course, that both gowns come from the same designer). And don't be afraid to ask to have embellishments like bows and beads added or removed, either. Keep in mind, though, that the more you stray from the original design, the more it will cost you in the end.

SELECTING COLOR  You'll also have to select your gown color. Believe it or not, there is more than one shade of white to choose from. There's stark white (the brightest, crispest white, usually found in synthetic fabrics), natural (a shade warmer than stark white), ivory (white with yellow undertones, also referred to as "eggshell" or "candlelight"), and champagne (a warm shade of white with pink undertones). A few of the hues can even be used together to produce different effects. For example, a stark white dress can be lined in an off-white fabric to create a softer version. A surprisingly wearable option for many skin types? Lining a white organza gown in soft pink or coral. The key to finding your shade is as simple as knowing your skin tone.

If your skin is fair, you'll look best in yellow ivories and warmer natural colors. You should probably steer clear of stark white, though, as it may wash you out. If your skin is medium with pink undertones, opt for creamier colors. But if your skin is medium with yellow undertones, choose natural whites or champagne. And if your skin is dark, congratulations: Most shades of white will complement you. However, if you have yellow or olive undertones, stay away from yellow-ivory dresses; try stark white or champagne hues instead.

When trying on different shades in the salon, keep in mind that the samples have been subject to lots of handling and trying on, so while the fabric is "white," it may appear a shade off its actual color. Be sure to ask for a clean fabric swatch to place near your face before making your final decision.

FINDING "THE ONE" Speaking of final decisions, how *do* you know when you've found The One? If you have to be reassured that the dress you're considering looks great on you, ask yourself how much you really like it. Is this how you pictured yourself looking as a bride? Can you really see yourself walking down the aisle swathed in this gown? If not, take it off and move on. But if the gown passes muster, take a deep breath, smile at your reflection, and breathe a huge sigh of relief—your search is over!

# GOING COUTURE

What happens if you loved several of the designs you tried on in salons, but just couldn't quite zero in on the dress of your dreams? Find yourself a good couturier and have him or her create your vision.

So, what is "couture" exactly? A couture gown is one that's developed from scratch around your very own personality, vision, and body type; there will never be another gown exactly like it. The major difference between a couture gown and an off-the-rack garment—besides the fact that the former is based on the bride's own concept, while the latter was created by someone else—is the way it will fit. Since a couture gown is created for one specific bride, it will be built around her figure, and her figure alone.

## STEP ONE: THE CONSULTATION

The couturier will hold a consultation with you to discuss body type, personality, and style; understanding and designing around these three elements is what will make the gown unique. Once an overall style is agreed on, the appropriate fabric is chosen and about forty-five different body measurements are taken so the couturier can ensure a proper fit.

## STEP TWO: THE MUSLIN

Using your measurements as a guide, a muslin pattern is then created. The muslin is a copy of the gown around which the actual gown will later be developed. It's basically a test garment, which allows your couturier to fine-tune fit, modify design details, and adjust proportions. The fabric generally used is unbleached muslin, since it's inexpensive, readily available, and its bland appearance makes a good backdrop for evaluating the work in progress. It can be pinned, taken apart, and restitched, allowing your couturier to experiment with all the elements that add up to a successful gown: the shape and depth of the neckline, waistline, bodice, and so on. It can also be used to test out different linings and boning placements.

## STEP THREE: THE FITTINGS

At your first muslin fitting, be sure to wear your wedding-day shoes and undergarments, as your couturier will need to know how high your heel height will be and how your foundation garments lie in front and back. Changing your underpinnings later on will change the fit and shape of your gown.

Many dressmakers expect to do at least two muslin fittings, so don't despair if the fit isn't perfect on the first go-round. Now is the time to speak up if the neckline isn't how you imagined it or if the sleeves aren't falling just so. And don't worry if you want to make drastic changes—after all, that's why your couturier is working in muslin in the first place.

## STEP FOUR: THE GOWN

Once the muslin has been fitted and adjusted to your specifications, it is re-marked and taken apart so your couturier is left with a full set of pattern pieces that will then be used for cutting, marking, and fitting your gown fabric. In other words, the muslin now becomes the pattern for your actual wedding gown. The gown is then created and fitted precisely to your body (again, you'll have several garment fittings) so that there is no gaping, falling, or pulling.

A WORD ABOUT FABRICS: While some
manufacturers are price conscious, often
sacrificing fine fabrics to keep costs down,
the couturier's focus is on finding the
perfect fabric for each gown design, taking
the bride's body type into consideration.
The selected fabric must have the right
drape, the right texture, and the right
weight in order for the finished product to
be flawless. In general, couturiers work
with finer, subtler fabrics. And they do all
of their embellishment work—beading,
embroidery—by hand. As such, a couture
gown is usually two to three times more
expensive than the average off-the-rack
version (though it's usually around the
same price as a fine designer gown).
Remember, though, that we're talking
about a gown that no one else in the world
will own, one that's made to fit you and only
you. How can you put a price on that?

COUTURE SKETCH BY CAROLINA HERRERA

# YOUR ORDER

When you're ready to order your gown, the store will take your measurements: bust, waist, hips. Each manufacturer has its own measurement chart, and this is what the store will use to determine your size. Ask to see the chart so you can have a better understanding of the way it works. And make sure the correct size gets ordered, using your largest measurement as a guide.

Your wedding dress is an important investment, so don't be afraid to ask many questions before plunking down a deposit. If you don't know already, find out who designed the dress you're interested in buying. Then ask how long it will take for the gown to come in once your order's been placed. If you're planning to sit for a bridal portrait, will the shop let you borrow your gown for pictures, then return it to them for pressing so it will look fresh for the wedding?

Also be sure to find out what the store's return policy is. Since bridal gowns are custom-made, most salons put a no-return policy in their contracts; if you can get any money back, it probably won't be any more than 50 percent of the cost. You should also ask for a written alterations estimate at the time of purchase, since it's generally not included in the cost of your gown. If the store doesn't do its own alterations, ask the salesperson you've been working with to recommend a reputable seamstress. Finally, find out if you can pay with a credit card, then use one. For such a big purchase, you want to be able to dispute a payment if something goes wrong. With all the money you're spending (on your gown and on your wedding in general), you might want to consider getting a charge card with air miles to contribute toward your honeymoon.

Be sure to request a letter of agreement or receipt with the following critical points: your name, the salesperson's name, and contact information for both of you; your wedding date; the amount of your deposit; your balance and date due or payment schedule; the cancellation or refund policy; and a detailed description of your gown, including the designer or manufacturer's name, style number, color, fabric, and size ordered; any special requests (extra length, beading, and so on) and their costs; delivery date; total itemized price for dress, headpiece, and veil (if ordered at the same time); alteration estimate, and any other accessories or service (such as steaming) requested. Retain a copy for your files.

If you're getting married in a location other than where you are purchasing your gown, inquire about shipping options from the salon. Be sure to allow plenty of time for the gown to arrive at your wedding location so there are no close calls near the actual date.

# YOUR FITTINGS

Every dress needs alterations. That's because the size is generally ordered based on your largest measurement. So, if you've got a large bust and narrow waist, your dress is going to have to be fitted more precisely to your frame. Alterations can be as simple as taking in the waist a bit and shortening the hem, or as detailed as shortening the sleeves, taking in the bodice, or adding lace and beads. You will probably have at least two or three fittings, which you'll schedule with the store when you purchase your dress; more may be necessary, so leave ample time before the wedding.

YOUR FIRST FITTING Your first fitting usually takes place about six weeks before your wedding day. Just as when you were shopping, it's a good idea to bring one eagle-eyed friend or family member along for advice. Before you go, decide which accessories you want to wear with your dress, and buy or order them so you can bring them along and see how everything looks together.

For your purposes, this fitting is to ensure two main things: that your gown is the right size, color, and design (neckline, train, sleeves, and so on), and that your seamstress knows what she's doing. A seamstress will most likely have an assistant (who could be the salon salesperson or another member of the salon staff) who helps you get into your gown. The seamstress should then begin looking for places where your dress needs to be taken in, let out, shortened, lengthened, or otherwise altered—hence the term *fitting*.

While she's busy fitting your gown, take a close look at the way the material falls, how the waist feels, how the chest area fits, and so on. Is there any funny puckering, bunching, or bulging? Look closely at the stitching, embroidery, or beading. Does everything seem well sewn? Look in the three-way mirrors to view all angles, and ask for another hand-held mirror if necessary. Speak up if you see anything you don't like—or forever hold your peace. This is your time to be demanding.

The seamstress should be able to tell you why each problem exists, and what can be done to fix it. Of course, don't expect miracles. This is why trying on the sample gown is so important: so you will have an idea of what you will get. But you are also paying big bucks for this gown, and it is your prerogative to have as many fittings as it takes to get the perfect fit. On that note, don't forget to schedule your next fitting before you leave the salon.

# YOUR FITTINGS

YOUR SECOND FITTING Your second fitting should occur about a month before your wedding. Bring along your foundation garments, bridal shoes, jewelry, and any accessories you plan to wear on your big day. And if you're not quite sure which accessories to wear and which ones to leave home, bring along a Polaroid camera as well, so you can see how each option looks with your dress.

In addition, you'll want to make sure all your concerns from the first fitting have been addressed and fixed. Then, start walking around the salon. Can you move comfortably in your gown? Does it stay in one place as you move? Is there any obvious wrinkling, bunching, or pulling of material? If you have a full-length dress, you'll also want to make sure your hem skims the tops of your shoes. Once again, speak up if you see something that doesn't look right. If there *is* a problem, continue to schedule fittings until you are completely satisfied.

YOUR FINAL FITTING When the day of your final fitting arrives, ask your mom and maid of honor to come along so they can learn about your gown. Does it need bustling? Ask the salesperson to teach them how to do it. Complicated straps or buttons? Ditto. Also, now's the time to find out how to get rid of last-minute wrinkles. Should you use an iron? On what setting? Is steaming a better option? And what if you spill something on the gown? Are there certain products you should/shouldn't use?

When your final fitting is complete, schedule a date and time within two weeks of your wedding to pick up your gown. When that day arrives, try your gown on one last time, especially if it's been a while since your last fitting. We all know the ways stress affects our appetites, and you don't want any last-minute surprises.

# DRESS SHOPPING
# TIMELINE

### NINE TO TWELVE MONTHS BEFORE

- Start envisioning yourself in your wedding dress. Write down six adjectives that describe how you want to look and feel.
- Start learning the ins and outs of wedding gowns. Learn all the dress parts and determine which design elements will best complement your body.
- Define your gown personality. Browse through the thousands of options online and in magazines to find designers and dress styles you like. Save printouts and tear sheets of some of your favorites in an accordion folder to bring along to the bridal salons.
- Consider your wedding logistics: the time, place, formality, and season of your nuptials.
- Determine your gown budget: 10 percent of your overall wedding budget is a good guideline.

### EIGHT MONTHS BEFORE

- Call and make appointments at three or four salons, allowing at least two hours at each salon, plus time in between. Keep track of addresses, dates, and times, as well as the names and phone numbers of the people working with you.
- Decide whom to bring and invite them along.
- Make your first trip to each salon. Do not consider putting a deposit down yet. Do remember which designers looked best on you, rank them, and write down descriptions of the gowns with prices.

### SEVEN MONTHS BEFORE

- Narrow your dress choices and go for a second (or third or fourth!) salon visit. You can return as many times as you like. Also, try to make at least one trip on your own.
- At the salon, ask if the gown has coordinating accessories (veil or shawl) and try them on, too. Don't feel pressured to order anything: You still have time to look elsewhere for accessories.

### SIX MONTHS BEFORE

- Order your gown.
- Shop for shoes, underpinnings, headpiece, and veil.

## FIVE MONTHS BEFORE

- Call the salon to confirm the delivery date.
- Decide which accessories—jewelry, wrap, gloves, bag, and outerwear—you need.
- Send shoes to be dyed, if necessary.
- Shop for bridesmaids' attire.

## FOUR MONTHS BEFORE

- Order bridesmaids' attire.
- If you don't plan on using your regular hairdresser, make appointments to have consultations with potential candidates. Bring along pictures of hairstyles you like, even a picture of your veil and headpiece. Consider whether you want to wear your hair in an updo; discuss with the hairdresser about how long it will take to grow your hair out if it's too short for your desired look.

## THREE MONTHS BEFORE

- Reserve men's formalwear.
- Make consultation appointments with potential makeup artists; book the one you like.
- Book your hairdresser.
- Help Mom or Stepmom shop for her outfit.

## SIX WEEKS BEFORE

ONCE YOUR GOWN HAS ARRIVED:

- Make sure your shoes, underpinnings, headpiece, and veil have arrived.
- Have your first fitting.

## FOUR TO FIVE WEEKS BEFORE

- Have your second fitting.
- Continue to schedule fittings until you are completely satisfied.
- Make sure bridesmaids have their attire and accessories.

## THREE WEEKS BEFORE

- Schedule a day and time to pick up your dress from the salon.
- Make an appointment with your hairdresser to have a final trim, and do a trial run with your veil and headpiece.
- Do a trial run with your makeup artist.

## TWO WEEKS BEFORE

- Pick up your dress. Try it on one last time, just to be sure.
- Find a dry cleaner or gown-preservation service and make arrangements to have your gown dropped off after the wedding.

## THE DAY BEFORE

- Remove the plastic cover from your gown and do any necessary pressing or steaming.

# 4 | ACCESSORIES

So, you've found your dress. But this shopping trip of all shopping trips is far from over. From the foundation garments that will help your gown hug your body just so, to the headpiece or flowing veil that will add formality and drama, your accessories are the elements that can help complete your look.

In general, the style of your gown is the keystone for choosing these other accoutrements. But while complementary style is the central concern, wearability and comfort are also important. Shop for accessories with an eye toward the luxurious and well appointed, but be modest in your selections: Too many extras can detract from the beauty of your gown. Focus your accessory attention on what's most important to you. For example, you may opt for a simple circle of tulle as your head covering, but demand a to-die-for pair of pumps. Either way, the more ornate your gown, the more simple your accessories should be, and vice versa. And as far as the actual buying process is concerned, we suggest you start at the top and work your way down.

# VEIL & HEADPIECE

Ask any of your married friends about the moment they first felt like a bride, and they'll tell you it was when they put on their veil. There's just something about a wispy piece of floating white fabric that completes the transformation from daily persona to . . . the bride!

The history of the veil is culturally diverse, with many interpretations. One belief common among Christians, Jews, Moslems, and Hindus is that the wedding veil served to protect the bride, who was susceptible to the ever-present stares of evil spirits. The vestal virgins of Roman mythology wore veils as a sign of their devotion to Vesta, the Roman goddess of the hearth; as a result, the veil came to symbolize virginal purity. In Biblical tradition, the custom of veil wearing originated when Rebekah, working in her father's field, covered her head in modesty when she first saw Isaac approaching. American folklore tells of one of the first brides to don a veil: George Washington's daughter, Nellie, was sitting by a lace-curtained window when one of her father's aides walked by and fell in love with her lace-framed face. When the two married, Nellie re-created the effect by wearing a lacy veil, thereby starting a trend still prevalent in the West.

When it comes to topping it off, it could be said that there are two types of brides: "hair" brides and "veil" brides. Figuring out which one you are is as simple as knowing what's most important to you. Hair brides prefer the focus to be on their hairstyle. They are quite content to just tack on a veil behind their updo, then remove it after the ceremony. A veil bride, on the other hand, wants to keep her veil on at the reception. Veil brides like full veils, usually with some edging or ornamentation, and long veils with multiple layers and a blusher. For them, the hairstyle is secondary; it's necessary only as support for helping to pouf up their veil.

Your choice of veil depends largely on the style of wedding gown you choose, as well as your personality. Feeling royal? Opt for a cathedral-length stunner like Princess Diana's. Want something more hip and modern? Go short. Something with a period feel? Try a caged veil.

# VEIL & HEADPIECE

DO I NEED ONE? Before you start shopping, make sure a veil is appropriate for your wedding. Strict etiquette mavens consider veils inappropriate for second-time brides, though today's more modern re-marriers do opt for veils, though they usually skip the blusher. A veil is not always a standard prerequisite (though you should check with your officiant about any religious head-covering requirements).

Unless you have an ornate necklace or lots of other accoutrements, though, you're going to want something above your neck—even if it's as simple as a single flower or a bejeweled hairpin. Sparkling tiaras and glittery barrettes are just a few more of today's modern headpiece options. Historically, Spanish brides have worn mantilla veils and orange blossoms in their hair to symbolize fertility and happiness.

Headpieces—decorative hair accessories usually anchored to your veil—are chosen separately from veiling. Though the earliest brides said their "I dos" crowned with floral and herbal wreaths—which continue to be popular, particularly for outdoor and beach ceremonies—there are many other options for the bride today. Eastern Orthodox brides look forward to a crowning ceremony when they marry, during which both the bride and groom have ornate crowns placed on their heads; the crowns are blessed and exchanged three times, and when they are removed, the couple is officially married. Similarly, the Finnish bride wears a gold crown, which she places on the head of a bridesmaid—while blindfolded—during a reception dance. It is said the lucky maid will be the next to marry, much in keeping with the tradition of American brides tossing the bouquet.

In general, headbands and tiaras look great with any face shape and hairstyle. Backpieces, which sit at the back or crown of the head where they can be attached to a veil, add extra oomph to a bride's overall look without becoming an integral part of the hairstyle. Sparkly barrettes and small, decorated combs are lovely low-maintenance looks, while hats remain a great option for short-haired or second-time brides.

Some dresses are made with matching veils and/or headpieces, which can make the choice easy for you. If yours is not, try on several different options with your gown, experimenting with different placements and examining your look from every angle. Then test security by moving your head around. If the piece feels unstable, have your salon add a few bobby pin loops.

CHOOSING YOUR STYLE When searching for your veil, you'll want to choose a style that best suits your face shape. A great rule to keep in mind is: "Opposites attract." For example, a round full face benefits from a veil that falls along the sides of the face and works to help narrow it, while an oblong face needs a veil that adds width—maybe one of the fountain variety.

In addition to face shape, you'll also want to consider your body type. Generally speaking, if you are tall, you can wear a veil that is more commanding. But a very fluffy veil with a large pouf can overwhelm a petite bride. Instead, opt for a narrow-cut veil, which will create a vertical line, giving the illusion of added height. And if you have a thick waistline, steer clear of a full veil to the waist—a more flattering option is an asymmetrical veil that cascades varying lengths of tulle down the back, creating a softer effect. If possible, stand in front of a full-length mirror when trying on veils to ensure that the proportions are right. Examine each veil from all angles. Remember: One that suits you from the back may not flatter your face in the front.

If your dress is ornate, plan to wear a plain veil. A simple dress, however, can take either a long cathedral-length veil (for added ceremony pomp and formality), or one with lots of embellishment. Any embellishment, however, should start below where your dress ornamentation ends, so they don't compete with each other. The embellishments—pearls, crystals, sequins—don't need to match those on your dress, but they should be complementary. For instance, if your gown embellishment is clusters of sequins in an elaborate floral pattern on the bodice, a veil with just a sprinkle of the same sequins along the edges will carry the motif through beautifully.

TIPS AND TRICKS   Something else to keep in mind: Crystals reflect
light and often photograph better than rhinestones, which can look like black
dots in snapshots. Beware of ribbon trim around the edge of your veil, as
well. Though it may look cleaner than unfinished tulle, it may—depending
on its length—create a horizontal line across your middle, making you
appear shorter.

   Are you going to wear a blusher (a veil that covers your face) during your
ceremony? Make sure it's long enough to flip up and over your head for the
all-important kiss-the-bride moment. And if you plan to remove your veil after
the ceremony but want to keep your headpiece on, make sure they are attached
with Velcro or hooks for easy on-and-off. Keep in mind, though, that if you
remove your veil during the reception, it won't be in pictures of the cake cutting,
first dance, etc. Many brides wait until after the first dance. If you choose
to keep your veil on for the entire wedding and you're wearing a cathedral-
length veil, you may want to try a multilayered version with a fingertip-
length layer overtop, which can be worn on its own during the reception.

# FACE TYPES

OVAL     ROUND     OBLONG     HEART     DIAMOND     SQUARE     RECTANGULAR     TRIANGULAR

The key to choosing the right veil is to first identify your face shape. The basic shapes are oval, round, oblong, heart, diamond, square, rectangular, and triangular. The first four shapes are soft and curved, while the last four have more angles. To determine which category you fall into, pull your hair away from your face and study the outer edge.

OVAL   Your face is slightly longer than it is wide, with curved soft edges. Basically, almost any veil will look good on you, as long as it complements your gown, neckline, and proportions.

ROUND   Your face has equal distance all around with the nose as a center point. It's as wide as it is long, with rounded edges. A round, full face will benefit from a veil that falls along the sides of the face and works to help narrow it. A round-faced bride should also stay away from round hairstyles. Wearing your hair down or in a face-framing bob is the best option.

OBLONG   Your face looks like an elongated oval. Many oblongs are mistaken for ovals, but placed next to a true oval you can see that an oblong has more length. If you have an oblong face, complement it with a bit of width. Look for veils of the fountain variety, paired with a wide tiara, wreath, or bun wrap. Stay away from piled-high hair, which will only add to the illusion of elongation.

HEART   Your face is wider at the eye, temple, and cheek area, with a narrow chin. The edges are soft and curved. If your face is heart-shaped, you'll want to add width at the jawline. Most veils will be too full for you. The best choice is a backpiece where the width shows up behind the neckline. As for hair, a chignon or flipped-up bob is a great look.

DIAMOND   Your face is widest at the cheeks and narrow at the chin and forehead, with sharp features. In other words, you're symmetrical, so your choices are limitless, as long as they complement your gown, neckline, and proportions.

SQUARE   Your face is basically straight across at the forehead and down the sides. Your jaw is strong and square, and your chin may stick out a bit. If the distance from the top of your face to your chin matches the width, you have a square face. A square jawline needs softness, so a longer veil will work better than a short, wide one. Many people consider a strong jawline a striking feature, however, and the confident bride will want to show it off.

RECTANGULAR   Your face is similar to a square, but longer than it is wide. Opt for longer veils to soften up the jawline, and pair with a wide tiara for added width.

TRIANGULAR   Your face is wider at the jaw and more angular than a heart shape, with a pointy chin. Try a veil that's fuller on top to balance the bottom half of your face.

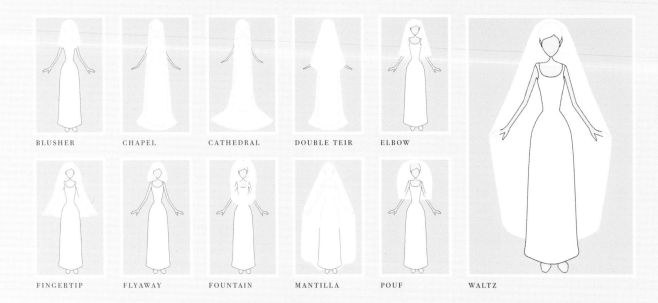

BLUSHER     CHAPEL     CATHEDRAL     DOUBLE TEIR     ELBOW

FINGERTIP     FLYAWAY     FOUNTAIN     MANTILLA     POUF     WALTZ

**BLUSHER** A short, single layer of veiling, the blusher is worn over the face before the ceremony, then either flipped over the head or removed thereafter.

**CHAPEL** A formal veil that extends to the floor, the chapel falls 2 ½ yards from the headpiece. The veil is often worn in combination with a sweep train and blusher.

**CATHEDRAL** The mother of all veils, the cathedral is the most formal. Sometimes referred to as the "royal" veil, this style falls 3 ½ yards from the headpiece.

**DOUBLE TIER** A veil of two layers (either two veils or a veil and a blusher), usually of different lengths.

**ELBOW** As the name implies, this type of veiling extends 25 inches in length to the bride's elbows.

**FINGERTIP** A very popular length, particularly with ball gowns, this style extends to the fingertips.

**FLYAWAY** A multilayered veil that just brushes the shoulders. Considered less formal than other styles.

**FOUNTAIN** This veil is gathered at the crown of the head to create a cascading effect around the face. Usually of shoulder or elbow length.

**MANTILLA** A long, Spanish-style, circular piece of lace that frames the face. Made either of lace or lace-edged tulle, the mantilla is usually secured with a comb.

**POUF** A gathered piece of tulle or netting that fastens to a comb or headpiece to create height for the veil.

**WALTZ** A veil length that falls somewhere between the knee and the ankle.

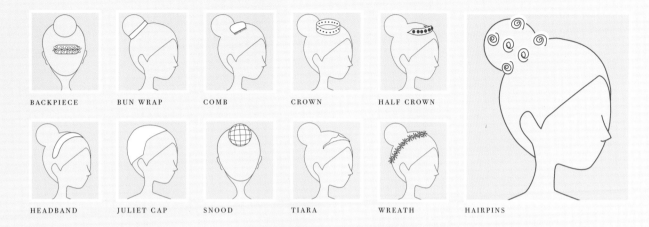

BACKPIECE   BUN WRAP   COMB   CROWN   HALF CROWN

HEADBAND   JULIET CAP   SNOOD   TIARA   WREATH   HAIRPINS

**BACKPIECE** A barrette or comb that fastens to the back of the head, to which the veil is then attached; the backpiece is often decorated with flowers, beads, or bows.

**BUN WRAP** Fairly self-explanatory, the bun wrap is a band that encircles a bun or an updo.

**COMB** As the name implies, this type of headpiece is held to the head with comb teeth for extra security. Can either be attached to a veil and worn on top of the head, or adorned with flowers and beads and used to cap an updo.

**CROWN** Different from a tiara, a crown is a full circular piece that sits atop the head and is adorned with stones, gems, or beads.

**HALF CROWN** Smaller than a crown, but greater in height than a tiara, the half crown is a half circle of jewels that sits atop the head.

**HEADBAND** A band of varying widths that closely follows the shape of the head.

**JULIET CAP** A small round cap that fits snugly on top of the head, usually decorated with pearls or semiprecious stones.

**SNOOD** A knitted or openwork net that encases the hair at the back of the head.

**TIARA** The headpiece of the moment, a tiara is a jeweled or beaded semicircle worn on top of the head.

**WREATH** A romantic, organic look the wreath—also known as the "garland"—features a full circle of flowers, twigs, foliage, and/or ribbon resting on the crown of the head.

**HAIRPINS** Bejeweled or enameled pins that can be worn alone or scattered throughout a hairstyle for an all-over glittery look.

# GLOVES

## SOMETHING OLD, NEW, BORROWED, BLUE

The tradition of the bride wearing something old (for continuity), new (for optimism about the future), borrowed (for borrowed happiness), and blue (for fidelity, good fortune, and love) on her wedding day stems from an Old English rhyme: "Something old, something new, something borrowed, something blue, a sixpence in your shoe." American custom has dropped the addition of the coin in the shoe, but many English brides still tote the sixpence underfoot.

Some brides consider their dress to be their something new, but here are a few options for the other three requirements.

SOMETHING OLD: A family heirloom, such as your grandmother's wedding band or string of pearls; a lace handkerchief; an old hat pin secured on the inside of your gown.

SOMETHING BORROWED: The headpiece or veil belonging to a family member or friend; a piece of your mother's jewelry.

SOMETHING BLUE: Your garter; blue toenail polish; lingerie.

During the eighteenth and nineteenth centuries, gloves were the traditional wedding favor for all guests. Until 1960, they were considered de rigueur, even during the day, for all well-mannered ladies. While today, formal etiquette still recommends that a bride wear gloves as a symbol of grace, they are not a requirement—many brides opt to do so simply to heighten the image they're presenting. The effect, when worn with a wedding dress, is classically elegant.

Gloves come in all lengths, expressed in terms of buttons (even if they have none). A one-button glove is wrist length. Four-, six-, and eight-button styles all stop below the elbow, and sixteen-button gloves are the most formal style, covering most of the upper arm. Gloves are also available in a variety of fabrics: silk, satin, lace, cotton eyelet, knit, even leather. And many feature trims that you can match to details on your dress. Again, a little embellishment goes a long way. So, if your gown features elaborate lacing on the bodice, just a simple touch of the same pattern on your gloves will do the trick.

TIPS AND TRICKS   Some general guidelines: Wear over-the-elbow gloves with a strapless or tank-style gown, elbow-length gloves with cap-sleeve gowns, and wrist-length gloves with short-sleeved gowns. If you're wearing a long-sleeved dress, skip them altogether. And if you have issues with your upper arms, avoid over-the-elbow styles and opt for elbow-length instead.

As for the all-important exchange of rings, the glove-wearing bride has two options. The first is to gently tug at the tip of each finger of your left hand, then slowly slide the glove off and hand it to your maid of honor. The other option is to carefully unstitch the seam of the ring finger ahead of time so there's a small opening. During the ring swap, slip your finger out. Once your band is in place, slide it gently back in. Either way, be sure to practice beforehand.

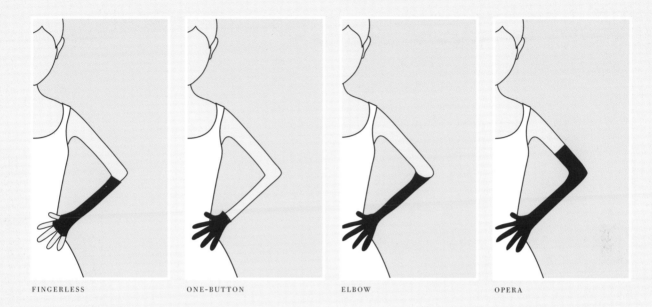

FINGERLESS          ONE-BUTTON          ELBOW          OPERA

FINGERLESS The fingerless glove—worn either short or long on the arm—is characterized by the absence of covered fingers. Some styles come to a point at and loop over the middle finger, while others are merely attached to the thumb. Great for the all-important exchange of rings.

ONE-BUTTON Most appropriate for informal or semiformal events, the hemline of a short glove ends within 2 inches of the wrist (about 9 inches long). This style looks great with long-sleeved gowns. Two- and four-button styles end between the wrist and the elbow.

ELBOW A glove that ends just above or below the elbow, this style can feature six, eight, or ten buttons, depending on the length of your arm.

OPERA The most formal of all gloves, the opera-length style (originally characterized by sixteen buttons) extends to the upper part of the bicep and looks wonderful with sleeveless and strapless gowns.

# UNDERPINNINGS & HOISERY

Though it may come as a surprise, what you wear under your gown is just as important to your overall look as the style of the gown itself. The proper underpinnings—bras, bustiers, slimmers—and hosiery can improve shape and fit, as well as increase your comfort level and lend overall support. When shopping for these items, the most important thing is comfort—attractive but functional are good words to keep in mind. You're going to be in that wedding gown ensemble for a minimum of five hours, and all eyes will be on you. To avoid unbridelike fidgeting and tugging, get the right size, shape, and style of underpinnings and hosiery for your body. Don't wear anything you've never tried before; practice wearing everything around the house first.

Try to bring as many of these items to your fittings as possible (your salon will tell you what you absolutely *must* bring along) to ensure you've made a good match. Can you see the boning of that bustier beneath the clingy fabric of your gown? Are those control tops visibly cutting your torso in half? Is the outline of your garter belt or your pantyhose waistband embarrassingly obvious? If so, rethink your options and consider other alternatives before the big day.

BRAS & BUSTIERS  If your gown is designed in such a way that you can wear a regular bra (such as a dress with sleeves, a sleeveless V-neck, or a bateau neck), you might wish to do so. Choose a strapless bra if your dress is strapless (obviously) or has very thin straps. A backless bra that hooks at the waist is best for a low-dipping or halter-style gown. If it's extra cleavage you seek, go for a push-up bra. And for the smoothest lines, opt for a body stocking with hose.

As you're trying on different pieces, remember that comfort is key. Many bras and bustiers are beautiful to look at, but you'll want to make sure that they feel good, too. Take note of any wires that are cutting into you, and be sure you're getting the proper support. Also watch out for over-embellished lacy or beaded designs, which may show through the fabric of your gown. And beware the wayward bra strap: If your gown doesn't have special strap-holding threads sewn into the bodice, have them sewn in or try double-stick tape underneath the straps to hold them in place.

# UNDERPINNINGS & HOSIERY

**SLIMMERS** If you're interested in resculpting your body, you may want to opt for a contemporary slimming device made with Lycra and/or Spandex—a popular alternative to the old-fashioned girdle your mother may have worn. Heralded for their lifting, nipping, and tucking capabilities, slimmers have become lifesavers for the modern sheath-wearing bride. An all-in-one slimmer is also good if you desire the support of control-top hosiery but wish to go bare-legged. A slimmer will give your figure a slightly different shape, so wear it for your first fitting.

**HOSIERY** When it comes to hose, you'll need to consider the style of your dress and shoes, and whether you desire any additional support. If you're going for the Cinderella experience in a full ball gown, your options are many, from sheer-to-waists to control tops and even to knee-highs. Wearing a form-fitting sheath? Opt for the slimming effects of control-top or body-shaping hose. These come in varying degrees, so find the level that achieves the desired effect without cutting off your circulation. For a clingy gown, think thigh-highs (if you're biologically blessed with lithe limbs) or seamless hose, which won't produce lines under body-hugging fabric. These may also be the best choice for gowns with a dropped or Basque waist, a style that may prohibit the sometimes obvious presence of a pantyhose waistband. Also, the friction of a built-in crinoline against your legs may shred your hosiery, so do a test run at your fitting and walk around in your gown. If your dress is casual or if you don't mind bare legs, you may choose to forgo hosiery completely, depending on the season.

If you wish to wear sandals or open-toed shoes and prefer the comfort of hose, look for a sandalfoot (also known as sandaltoe) style with a sheer toe. Also, try to pick a shade of hose complementary to your gown. A popular choice is sheer hosiery for a sleek, sexy look. Many styles are virtually invisible against the leg, and are available in a variety of subtle tints or with hints of gold or ivory. Looking for a little sex appeal? Be bold and go for glimmer with hosiery that has a slight sparkle or sheen to it. Avoid opaque hosiery, though, as its less-see-through appearance seems heavy and fails to really accentuate the lines of the leg.

One final word: To avoid the inevitable underwear wedgie—which is pretty much impossible to fix in a wedding gown—wear pantyhose with a sewn-in cotton crotch, or thong underwear. If you've never worn a thong, try one first—this barely-there item is not for everyone.

## THE GARTER

The origins of the garter toss are humorous: It began in medieval times, when silk sashes were tied below the bride's knees and guests would literally rip them off for luck—and to hasten the consummation process. To defend herself, the bride eventually began to throw her garter to her guests! These days, the groom removes the garter—generally worn at the sexier mid-thigh level—from her leg (as innocently as possible, we're sure) and tosses it to his bachelor pals. It used to be believed that the lucky guy who caught the garter would inherit some of the bride and groom's good fortune. Nowadays, he either keeps it as a souvenir or is made to place it on the leg of the woman who caught the bride's bouquet.

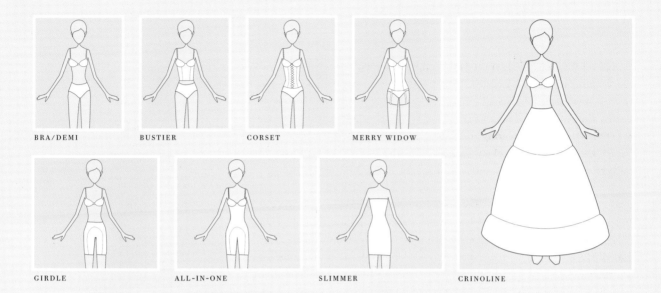

BRA/DEMI    BUSTIER    CORSET    MERRY WIDOW

GIRDLE    ALL-IN-ONE    SLIMMER    CRINOLINE

BRA/DEMI  A shaped undergarment that molds and supports the breasts. The bra is the *über*-undergarment, that leading piece of lingerie to which all others play supporting roles. Variations include long-line bra-girdles with boning and underwire; push-ups; backless bras; minimizers; and demi-cup bras, which expose the upper part of the breasts, for wear with low necklines.

BUSTIER  A tight-fitting, often strapless, waist-length combination bra and waist cincher, held in place by boning, elastic, or stretch knit fabrics.

CORSET  A sleeveless, boned foundation garment laced up the front or back to shape the figure.

MERRY WIDOW  A bustier that extends below the waist and has garter straps attached for wear with stockings.

GIRDLE  An undergarment designed to mold the lower torso and upper legs.

ALL-IN-ONE  A bra and girdle combined into a one-piece foundation garment.

SLIMMER  A smooth undergarment that uses Lycra or Spandex to "resculpt" the body; available for the tummy, legs, even buttocks.

CRINOLINE  A stiff petticoat or underskirt made to hold out full skirts and give them their fullness.

# SHOES

Of course you want your wedding shoes to be unabashedly beautiful, but you also want them to feel good on your feet. While we hate to admit it, comfort is ultimately critical: Nobody wants to see a bride hobbling around after the first dance. And let's face it—you won't be spending much time sitting down, so if your feet hurt, you're bound to be miserable. Low-heeled pumps are probably the best option. If you're pining for higher heels, try not to go too high; 2 inches is a good benchmark. Otherwise, you may stumble on one of the layers of your gown, your legs will be quicker to tire, and if you're marrying outdoors, you may end up with two sticks in the mud.

Strange, but true: If you're planning to wear shoes not specifically designed for weddings, the best time to shop is about a year before your big day, because that's when shoes that suit the season will be shown. Of course, you'll need to purchase your wedding gown first. But once that's chosen, shoes should be your next stop, as you'll need them for your fittings.

Many brides use their shoes as an outlet for expressing personal style, opting for everything from fur-trimmed bridal boots to saucy stilettos. Other more conventional styles include square- or round-toed pumps, strappy sandals, ballet slippers, and slingbacks. For the most formal affairs, bridal shoes should be silk or satin. Most are available in different shades of white or are dyeable, so you can match them perfectly to your gown—though today, metallic shoes like silver and gold have become standard alternatives, as have those with touches of pale blue beading. And again, opposites attract. While a simple dress looks great with stand-out shoes, if your gown features beading and lace on the hem, you'll want to stick with simplicity.

TIPS AND TRICKS   If you have the time, break in your shoes before the big day, but do it indoors on clean floors to avoid dirt and grass stains. Another good idea is to buy your shoes a little big, then place insoles in the top half and remove them as your feet swell during the course of the evening. You should also scuff the bottoms of your shoes to avoid wedding wipeouts—even scratching them up with the rough edge of a key will suffice—and you can even stretch them out a bit, if need be, by wearing them around the house with sweat socks.

## LUCKY ACCESSORIES

In addition to their classic accessories—jewelry, veil, shoes—brides the world over have traditionally toted good-luck charms on their wedding day in an effort to secure a favorable union and future prosperity. Here are some of the more potent possibilities, past and present.

ANCIENT GREECE AND ROME: Roman brides carried bunches of herbs, most often rosemary, to symbolize fidelity, fertility, and to scare off evil spirits. The Greeks carried ivy, symbolizing eternal love.

ENGLAND: The bride courts luck by carrying a decorated horseshoe on her arm down the aisle and/or sewing a silver horseshoe charm into the hem of her gown. She also tucks a sixpence in her shoe.

GERMANY: The bride carries salt and bread in her pocket to ensure bounty, while her groom carries grain, for wealth and good fortune.

BELGIUM: Traditionally, a bride is given a handkerchief with her name embroidered on it to carry in her sleeve or bodice; afterward, she may have it framed and hung in a prominent spot in her new home.

SWEDEN: The bride wears a silver coin from her father in her left shoe and a gold coin from her mother in her right shoe.

GREECE: A bride often carries a small pair of scissors in her bridal bouquet to "cut" the evil eye.

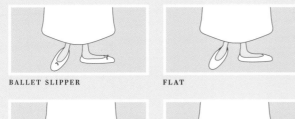

BALLET SLIPPER FLAT

MARYJANE

MULE

PUMP SANDAL ANKLE STRAP SLINGBACK

BALLET SLIPPER A flat, soft satin shoe that resembles a slipper; some feature ribbons that wind around the ankle.

FLAT A shoe with a heel height of less than ½ inch.

MARYJANE A round-toed shoe with a single strap across the instep.

MULE A slip-on shoe without a back strap or Achilles support.

PUMP A closed-toe, slip-on shoe with a medium to high heel.

SANDAL An open-toe shoe with straps across the toes, of various heel heights.

ANKLE STRAP A shoe with a strap that fastens around the ankle.

SLINGBACK A shoe with a strap at the back that fastens across the Achilles tendon.

# BOUQUET

It may seem a bit odd to think of your bridal bouquet as a fashion accessory, but since you will be carrying it the first time your groom—and all the guests—see you, you'll want to coordinate it with your ensemble and the rest of your wedding. After all, it's going to be the most in-the-spotlight accessory.

The bouquet you choose should highlight and balance your overall look: It shouldn't be overpowering, or unmanageable. Small round clusters of flowers (known as nosegays) are easy to carry and look great with almost any gown. Big gowns need the balance of profuse nosegays and denser bunches of blooms, like the round bouquet (in which lots of flowers are wired or hand-tied), the cascade (a waterfall-like spill of blooms), and the pageant (also known as the presentation, a longer, hand-tied bouquet with stems showing, carried sideways, draped over the forearm—think beauty-pageant winner). Sheaths and short dresses, meanwhile, look best with smaller sprays or single stems.

TIPS AND TRICKS   When choosing your flowers, keep in mind that you want them to reflect the overall tone of your wedding, whether modern or traditional. But if your dress is simple, don't be afraid to go bold in color or style.

Whatever you choose, make sure your blooms are grander than those carried by your attendants. Their bouquets should showcase yours by complementing its color and shape, not overpowering it.

ROUND

CASCADE

PRESENTATION/PAGEANT

SPRAY

NOSEGAY

ROUND  A dense bunch of blooms anchored in a bouquet holder, wired, or hand-tied.

CASCADE  A waterfall-like spill of blooms and greenery anchored in a handheld base.

PRESENTATION/PAGEANT  A grand bouquet of flowers with long stems, tied with ribbon and carried in the arms, pageant-style.

SPRAY  A loosely hand-tied bunch of blooms of irregular length and height.

NOSEGAY  A small round cluster of flowers, all cut to uniform length. Usually made with one dominant flower or color, wrapped tightly with ribbon or lace.

# BRIDESMAIDS

Okay, so they're not exactly accessories, but tradition dictates that maids dress to complement the bride. If your attendants complain about having to wear the exact same thing (although these days, of course, they don't have to match), tell them this: Keeping evil spirits away from the couple on their wedding day is a recurring theme in wedding tradition, and bridesmaids used to wear the exact same outfit as the *bride* so that the spirits would be confused as to just who the actual to-be-wed was.

Nowadays, maids can dress in any number of styles—A-line gowns, sheaths, two-piece ensembles, and Empire-waist gowns—though their overall look should still coordinate well with the bride's. For example, if the bride is wearing an elegant full-length gown, her bridesmaids shouldn't be dressed in knee-length sundresses. In general, the maids' dresses should never be longer than the bride's. Likewise, they should never be more elaborate. Which means if, for example, the bride's gown is simple, matte, and understated, her maids shouldn't be waltzing down the aisle in a number that's super-shiny and intricately embellished.

The easiest way to coordinate the maids' dresses with your own is to pick up on a single detail in your bridal gown—a piece of lace, a hint of color, the cut of the neckline—then search for bridesmaid dresses with a similar style.

TIPS AND TRICKS   The best place to start your search is the Internet, where you can view hundreds of styles and sort them based on price, style, designer, and color before hitting the stores. Most bridal salons also carry bridesmaid dresses, as do many evening-wear and department stores. The best time to start shopping for bridesmaid dresses is six months before the wedding, as it'll take a few months for the dresses to come in if they're custom-ordered, and you'll want to be sure there's time to deal with alterations and any possible problems.

When you do start shopping, it's probably best to go it alone your first time out, so you can get a sense of what's out there, or bring along just one maid or your honor attendant to have her test-drive a few different looks. On a later trip, try to bring along all your maids, so they'll feel like they have a say in what's chosen—which may mean fewer hassles for you in the long run.

# HAIR
## AND MAKEUP

You want to hire professionals but don't know where to start? Ask friends who've had their hair and makeup done for big events, and inquire at your local hair salon or at the cosmetic counters of area department stores. You might also ask your wedding-day photographer, bridal salon, or wedding consultant for suggestions.

After you've garnered a few names, you'll want to conduct phone interviews to find out about their experience. Have they worked on many weddings? Can they show you pictures of their work? How much do they charge for a consultation? What is the fee for taking care of you, and possibly your mom and bridesmaids, on your wedding day? Can they stay for touch-ups during the photo session? Will they travel?

Once you've gotten the answers you're looking for, book an appointment for a consultation. Bring along photos or magazine pages of looks you favor. For the hairstylist, you'll want to wear something in the same shade as your wedding gown, with a similar neckline if possible; bring along a photo of your veil and/or headpiece, so the stylist knows what to expect. Ask the stylist to photograph each finished look from four different angles—front, back, and sides—and to write down the products and techniques used. For makeup artists, bring along your own cosmetics so the stylist can get an idea of the colors you like; if you're happy with the look he or she creates for you, take a few photographs to document it, and write down which products were used so you can purchase the same products for your wedding.

Your hair and makeup stylists may require a deposit to save the date; be sure to request a receipt or have them sign a formal contract detailing everything you expect on the big day. They can be hired in different ways: You go to their salon; they come to you and do you, your mom, and your bridal party; or, budget permitting, they can come and stay with you throughout the day to do touch-ups before the photo session and the ceremony.

# THE GROOM

Think the only person people pay attention to at a wedding is the woman in white? Guess again. The groom's clothing will be on view too, even though it will depend largely on your attire and the time and location of your event. Don't stress too much, though, about matching. Just because your gown has lilac embroidery doesn't mean your groom needs to wear a lilac tie. Sometimes, all it takes is a hint of the same hue in his boutonniere to create a unified look.

You should, however, make sure your ensembles are coordinated in terms of formality. For example, if your wedding is a semiformal, daytime affair and you're wearing an ankle-length dress with flirty floral embroidery, your groom should skip the tux and opt for a suit (navy or charcoal are great year-round; reserve khaki or white for warm seasons) and a white shirt worn either with or without a tie.

If your wedding is a semiformal, evening affair, and you're clad in a sexy sheath, have him don a dark tuxedo and bow tie, worn with a cummerbund or vest, or a nice dark suit. Either way, his shirt should be white, with a wing-tipped or turned-down collar. For summer weddings or tropical locales, white dinner jackets are an acceptable option. On the other hand, if your wedding is a formal, daytime affair, tuxedos and morning coats are appropriate, paired with a white spread-collar shirt, a vest, and an ascot or four-in-hand tie.

For a formal, evening affair, when you're dressed to impress in a full ball gown, it's time for your groom to break out the black tie. That means a classic black tuxedo with a white wing- or spread-collar shirt, black bow tie, and matching vest or cummerbund. Formal four-in-hand ties are also a more contemporary option for the fashion-forward groom. If your wedding falls during the summer, a white dinner jacket with formal trousers is another option. And finally, if your wedding is ultra-formal, have your groom dress in white tie. That means a tailcoat, trousers, white piqué wing-collared shirt, black vest or cummerbund, and white bow tie. For extra pizzazz, make your wedding gift to him a fancy set of studs and cuff links.

# THE GROOM

TIPS AND TRICKS  If your groom already owns a tuxedo and plans to wear it for the wedding, be sure to take a good look at it. Is it in style? Is it the right weight for the wedding? Does it fit him properly? If not, he should shop for a new one. If your groom is excited by the notion of checking out all of his formalwear options—and there are many—great! But if not, you'll need to escort him to a tux rental or formalwear shop to be measured, and take it from there.

For most grooms, renting a tuxedo will probably suffice. But don't wait until the last minute, or all the best tuxes will be gone. Reserve all formalwear around the three- or four-month mark. Call a few chain and independent tuxedo shops ahead of time to make appointments and find out their rental price range, what they have in stock, and what kind of package deals they offer.

If, however, your groom has reason to wear a tux again in the future, it may be worth buying one. Look at it this way: Renting costs about 25 to 30 percent of the price of a new tuxedo. So, if he attends three or four formal events a year, it's worth it to buy. And as long as it's a classic style—two- or three-button jacket with medium-sized lapels—he'll be able to wear it time and time again.

## GROOM CHECKLIST

- [ ] Tux/suit
- [ ] Tie
- [ ] Ascot
- [ ] Shirt
- [ ] Vest/cummerbund
- [ ] Socks
- [ ] Shoes
- [ ] Undershirt
- [ ] Boxers/briefs
- [ ] Cuff links
- [ ] Studs
- [ ] Suspenders
- [ ] Tie tack

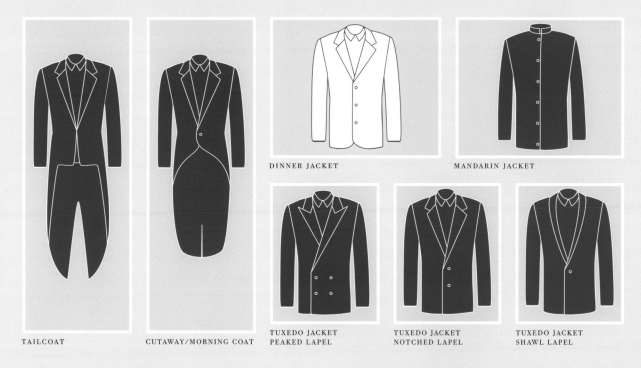

TAILCOAT

CUTAWAY/MORNING COAT

DINNER JACKET

MANDARIN JACKET

TUXEDO JACKET
PEAKED LAPEL

TUXEDO JACKET
NOTCHED LAPEL

TUXEDO JACKET
SHAWL LAPEL

TAILCOAT Also known as full dress or tails, this jacket has a two-button single-breasted front or six-button double-breasted front; it is short in front with two long tails in the back. It is usually black, but is sometimes seen in white. A tailcoat is generally worn at ultra-formal evening weddings with a white waistcoat and bow tie.

CUTAWAY/MORNING COAT Worn for formal daytime weddings (11 A.M. to 4 P.M.), this coat is short in the front, long in the back, and tapers from the front waist button to a wide back tail. These jackets are either black or charcoal gray and are worn with gray pinstripe or matching gray trousers and the formal ascot tie.

DINNER JACKET This tuxedo-style jacket is white or ivory. A dinner jacket is great for both formal and semiformal evening affairs during spring and summer.

MANDARIN JACKET Also called a Nehru or Mao jacket, the mandarin jacket has a standup collar and no lapels. It is worn with a Mandarin-collared shirt, which makes wearing a tie obsolete. The single-breasted jacket generally has six buttons, with the first button at the top of the placket.

TUXEDO JACKET The tux jacket can be single-breasted (with a one- to four-button front) or double-breasted (with a two- to six-button front). The jacket is worn for formal or semiformal evening events with matching trousers, which may have a satin stripe down the outside of the leg. The tux is generally worn with a bow tie and vest or cummerbund.

LAPEL STYLES Peaked: A broad lapel that points upward in a wide V at the collar. Notched: A lapel with a triangular indention where it meets the collar. Shawl: A smooth, rounded lapel with no notch.

# 5 | DRESSING

**Your dress** has been fitted to total perfection. Your groom has survived the bachelor party, and your mom has had her last good cry. What's it all mean? That after months of planning, it's finally time to say "I do." The most important thing you can do at this stage in the game is to be prepared, stop stressing, and go with the flow. Use this chapter as a guide to the final steps leading up to the morning when you wake up and realize, "I'm getting married today."

# PRE-WEDDING PREP

The first thing to consider is where you want to get ready on your wedding day. Will you dress at home? At your ceremony site? At your parents' house? Some other locale? And will your family and bridal party be dressing in the same place, or somewhere else?

A week or two before the wedding, do a dry run of your hair and makeup, confirm all your appointments, and set a schedule for yourself on your wedding day. Let's face it—everything comes down to timing. Which means all of your hair and makeup appointments (and those of your wedding party) need to occur at precisely the right moments.

Here's how to figure out your timetable: Ask your photographer what time you'll need to be ready for photos, and ask your stylist how long it will take for hair and makeup. Then count backwards, giving yourself an extra half hour. For example, if photos are scheduled for 4 P.M., make sure everyone involved—you, your groom, your parents, the wedding party—is ready to go by 3:30.

If your stylist is coming to you, make sure the space you'll get dressed in has a vanity table or low counter with a mirror. Check to see that your chair has a low back, so your stylist will have easy access to your head. And make sure there are electrical outlets nearby for appliances like hair dryers, curling irons, and electric rollers. Bring a few extension cords just to be safe.

Once you've got all the logistics down, it's time to pack your gown emergency kit and start packing for your honeymoon. Finally, on the day before your wedding, remove the plastic cover from your gown, inspect it thoroughly for loose threads or buttons, do any necessary pressing or steaming, and lay out all your accessories.

When you wake on the big day, take a long shower or bath, do some stretches, drink lots of water, and eat a healthy breakfast that will keep you energized throughout the day. Give your gown emergency kit to your maid of honor. Put your undergarments and hosiery on under a white button-front shirt or robe (the stand-in for your white gown) so you'll be ready to slip on your dress when your hair is done and your headpiece and veil are in place. Then have your hair and makeup done before you dress. (You may also want to take a moment to brush your teeth before your lipstick is applied.)

If the stylist has finished handling your tresses and you don't like the way you look, or if your makeup isn't exactly the way is was in your dry run, be honest. Make cheerful suggestions about how you'd like to change things. Or ask your maid of honor to pipe up for you. Work with your stylists to make the needed

- [ ] Dress
- [ ] Veil
- [ ] Headpiece
- [ ] Shoes
- [ ] Hose
- [ ] Bra/bustier
- [ ] Slip/petticoat
- [ ] Slimmer
- [ ] Underwear
- [ ] Garter
- [ ] Gloves
- [ ] Jewelry
- [ ] Purse

adjustments. And if your veil needs to be removed after the ceremony, ask your hairdresser to show your mom or honor attendant how to do it.

Before you step into your gown, you'll also want to wash your hands to avoid getting any smudges on the fabric (those who will help you get dressed should give their hands a good wash as well). Now is also a good time to take a last bite of food, a last sip of water, and to make a final trip to the bathroom.

PRESERVING YOUR GOWN Whether you decide to save your gown for your own daughter, rework it as a cocktail dress, or preserve it for posterity, the first thing you'll need to do post-wedding is to have it properly cleaned. Unseen champagne spills and perspiration can stain, and the longer you let stains sit, the harder it is to have them removed.

In the best-case scenario, you'll engage the services of an expert gown-cleaning and -preservation service as soon after your wedding as possible to prevent permanent damage to the fabric. And if you try to clean the stains yourself, you run the risk of setting them. On the other hand, don't assume there aren't any stains on your gown just because you can't see them. Some stains will dry clear, only to appear as brown spots later on when they chemically oxidize.

In the weeks leading up to your wedding, do an Internet search for "wedding gown preservation" to find experts in your area, and ask your married friends about their experiences. Then, call the establishments you're interested in and ask a lot of questions. Is this their primary business? Do they offer a written warranty? Can they give you a list of references? Will you be able to look at your dress after the process, or is it sealed in a box? (The latter is a big no-no, as it could expedite deterioration—if they answer yes to this, move on.) Also get a price estimate: Expect to pay from $100 to $150 at a dry cleaner, and from $250 to $500 for an expert preservation service.

After you've spoken with a few different companies, independently qualify them and choose the one you feel most comfortable with. If none of the establishments seem up to par, or if you're simply having trouble finding a trained professional, ask a local museum for a recommendation, or check with your bridal salon or the designer of your gown. If you still can't find an expert—or simply can't afford one—bring your gown to your local dry cleaner. Doing something is better than doing nothing. And a treasure as special as your wedding gown should be protected properly, so that a bride who wears it in the future will look as beautiful in it as you did.

# FAST FIXES

Getting dressed and got some makeup on your gown? Or ink on your sleeve? Or worse yet—got a prominent pimple? A little preparation—and a smartly packed emergency kit—can make a world of difference. (Note: These quick fixes may not entirely remove your spots and spills, but they will minimize them and make them easier to get out later. Please run over the details with your salon before trying any of the techniques listed below—each dress fabric is different, and therefore may react differently. Beware: Removing stains from your bridal gown can be a pretty tricky business. Water or liquid cleaner could leave a mark, and bleaches can irreparably burn the fabric.)

### SUDDEN SPOT

Wedding stress can wreak havoc on your skin. FAST FIX: Dot a red pimple with Visine (to get the red out), then add a touch of concealer as close to your skin tone as possible.

### BROKEN NAIL

You're not sure how you did it, but you snagged a nail. Immediately file it down so it doesn't snag your dress fabric. Or, if it's part of a major manicure job, apply a drop of glue to the break and position a tiny bit of unused paper from a tea bag on top, then add another drop of glue. When it dries, file the paper down until you can't see or feel the edges, then top with a third and final drop of glue.

### SWOLLEN EYES

Eyes a wreck from a day-before breakdown? FAST FIX: Flush your peepers with Visine, then relieve puffiness with cold tea bags— the tannin will help tighten swollen tissue.

### INK SPOT

Signing your ketubah or marriage contract and your hand slipped? FAST FIX: Apply a touch of hair spray to a cotton swab, then rub lightly over the stain.

### MAKEUP MESS

Spot a makeup smudge on your gown? Don't rub it. Press a little club soda onto the spot, then sprinkle salt on top to soak up the moisture. Let dry. If a hint of a spot remains, touch up with a cotton swab and talc.

### SHINY FACE

Come prepared with a small package of blotting papers, or keep a cotton handkerchief, loose powder, and big puff close at hand.

### WATERMARK

Tears of joy left a watermark on your gown? Attacking it with a hair dryer might spread the spot even further. FAST FIX: Run over it with a hand steamer to dissipate edges, then iron.

### OIL STAIN

Whether it's from your perfume or a small bite of salad, a splash of oil can quickly spoil a white gown. FAST FIX: Dip a cotton swab into cornstarch, white chalk, or talcum powder, then gently but generously apply it to the spot. Wait 15 minutes for the moisture to be absorbed, then blot with a white towel. Repeat if necessary.

### RED WINE

A guest spilled red wine on your gown? FAST FIX: Sprinkle salt on the spot to neutralize it, then blot with a clean towel.

### STOCKING RUN

If your legs are a central factor of your outfit, stash a couple extra pairs of hose in your purse or the ladies' room. Otherwise, a dab of clear nail polish will do the trick.

### BROKEN BUSTLE

In a pinch, extra-big safety pins can fix a bustle that has inadvertently been stepped on and torn.

# GETTING DRESSED

Know this: Getting dressed on your wedding day is at least a two-person job. When it's finally time to step into your gown, place a white sheet on the floor, put on your garter, unzip or unbutton your dress all the way down, and place your shoes on the floor underneath it. Have your mom or an attendant hold the dress open, then slowly step into it one leg at a time, placing your feet in your shoes as you do so. If you must slip your gown over your head (for example, if it's a sheath that simply can't be stepped into), use a scarf to cover your face so you don't end up with makeup smudges. If you have lots of buttons, have a crochet hook on hand to help pull the loops over them.

After your gown's been fastened, have your mom or maid reexamine you to make sure every button, loop, snap, and zipper has been secured, every inch of fabric is lying smoothly, and there are no last-minute smudges or spots. If you need to sit down for a moment before hitting the aisle, make sure it's on a backless stool with your gown fluffed out around you, not scrunched under you. If you can't find a backless stool, pull your gown up before you sit, and ask an attendant to drape your train over the back of the chair. And if you need last-minute face powder or a sip of water, be sure to drape a towel over the front of your bodice to catch any spills. Finally, turn toward a full-length mirror and take a long moment to look at yourself before heading out the door.

# BUSTLING AROUND

From ceremony to reception, you'll need to take care when moving around in your dress. If you're driving to different locations, get in and out of the car slowly, taking care to avoid greasy door locks, dirt, and dust. You should also avoid sitting on the back of your gown; pull it up behind you and sit forward instead. And if you're taking pictures outside, bring along a pillowcase so you won't have to sit or stand directly on the ground and suffer grass stains.

If you need to maneuver on stairs or cross the street, it's important that you gently lift your gown to avoid last-minute tears and stains. To do so, bend just a tiny bit at the knees and softly gather a piece of your skirt in each hand (if you carelessly grab a fistful of fabric, you'll cause your gown to wrinkle). Then slowly lift your skirt away from the ground. If your dress is full or designed with a train, try not to walk or step backwards (again, you'll risk ripping the fabric). Instead, reach behind you and delicately lift the back of your skirt. When you reach your destination, simply drop the skirt behind you, take your first few steps, and enlist the help of an attendant to fluff and arrange the fabric.

Unless you've chosen a trainless gown or one with a sweep or detachable version, you're going to want to bustle it after the ceremony (though some brides wait until after the first dance). Designate a bustler (usually a wedding consultant, family member, or honor attendant) and bring her with you to your last fitting so she can learn the ins and outs of your gown. Once you've been bustled on the big day, the entire hem of your gown should be even and the fabric should drape gracefully, but not so fully that you can't sit comfortably. And since going to the bathroom is also a two-person job, you may want to ask your bustler to pitch in here, too. Note to those of you in big ball gowns: Don't be shocked if you actually have to step out of your gown altogether for your trip to the toilet.

If you wait to bustle until after the first dance, you'll want your bustler to take charge of your train in the meantime. She'll need to help you in and out of the car, drape your train over your chair when you sit, and help transport it when you walk. Another option is to attach a loop to your train that you can slip over your wrist, allowing you to carry your own train all night.

When you get to your reception and start making the rounds, don't forget all that great advice your mom gave you—you know, stand up straight, keep your shoulders back, don't chew gum, watch your language, put your napkin in your lap, *smile.* Of course, that last one will probably come naturally. *Have fun.*

# GETTING UNDRESSED

The party was a success. How does a newly married woman go about getting out of her gown? For starters, know that since it took you so long to get into your dress—what with all the underpinnings and accessories and hooks and closures—it's going to take some time for you to get out of it. Which means you won't exactly be exiting your reception and jumping right into bed (that is, assuming you don't choose to change into street clothes at the reception site—a somewhat old-fashioned practice). To speed things up, enlist the help of your new hubby. Keep that crochet hook handy so he can help you undress without busting your buttons. But realize that since he's not your mom or honor attendant, your man may need a little guidance when it comes to unlacing, unbustling, and unhooking. Once you've successfully guided him through the process, remove your shoes and ask him to stand in front of you so you can lean on him while you slowly step out of your gown. And don't ignore that gorgeous heap you've just left on the floor. You want to enjoy it for years to come, don't you?

So what should you do? Pick up your dress gingerly and store it by wrapping it in a clean cotton sheet and laying it flat in a cool dark place, such as in a spacious closet or under the bed (just don't forget it's there!). You can even store it in a cotton pillowcase in a pinch. Simply let your gown fold into a soft pile, then place it in the case. Soft folds will wreak less havoc than sharp creases.

Whatever you do, don't wrap your dress in plastic. This can trap moisture, inviting mold and mildew. And if you hang your gown on an ordinary wooden or wire hanger, the weight of the dress will stretch and distort the weave of the fabric. If you prefer to hang your dress, use only a padded hanger. Keep your gown separate from your veil and other accessories to prevent the fabric from snagging. Don't expose it to direct sunlight, or it will fade and become discolored. It may be the last thing you want to think about on the eve of your wedding, but remember, just like anything else in life, the more energy you put into it now, the more enjoyment you'll reap in the future.

## ACKNOWLEDGMENTS

This book reflects the creativity, smarts, and dedication of the incredibly talented staff I have the good fortune of working with at The Knot. Jennifer Cegielski took the editorial reins to bring the manuscript to conclusion, and Amy Vinchesi masterfully managed every last wandering detail while making it all look easy. Hollee Actman Becker, talented fashion writer, did an amazing job pulling the disparate—and evolving—ideas together into a smooth-flowing story. Catarina Tsang, as always, provided impeccable creative vision for the look and structure. And, this book would not have been half of what it is without the illustrations of the supremely talented Amy Saidens. Thank you all—and everyone on staff who pitched in at times of need, particularly Elisa Prainito and Brittany O'Neil—for being so good at what you do.

Our editor at Chronicle, the savvy and supportive Mikyla Bruder, could not have been a better fit for this project. I thank her for her insight in helping us to unravel the puzzle that was the many elements of this book and for her incredible patience while guiding us through rewrites, edits, and deadlines. My thanks also to my former agent Jonathan Diamond, who dreamed up this book idea and directed it into the hands of the publisher who would best do it justice. And thanks, too, to our agent from RLR, Jennifer Unter, who ultimately dotted all of our i's and crossed our t's.

I owe my entire knowledge of bridal gowns to the brilliant group of designers who make up the world of wedding fashion today. We are honored to have the guidance of Carolina Herrera on our editorial advisory board. Many thanks to designers Melissa Sweet and Cynthia Corhan, who have had the patience to provide clear answers to my many crazy questions about construction and fabrics and fit. Thanks as well to all of the designers who have welcomed us at the market, have participated in *The Knot Wedding Gowns* magazine, and have taken the time to explain the intricacies of the gowns we have featured here.

I have several friends in the field to thank for many of the concepts in these pages: Henry and Michelle at Michelle Roth salon in New York City; Yolanda, of the famed Yolanda Enterprises outside of Boston; Jonas and Ursula Hegewisch of Wearkstatt in New York City; the California-based couturier Michael Jon; makeup artists Rochelle Weithorn and Morgen Schick DeMann; bridal consultants Gretchen Maurer and Marcy Blum; and Ilene Shack of Independent Visions. And, most importantly, a special thanks to all of the brides who have used The Knot to find their dresses and to plan the event of a lifetime.

And finally, thanks to my mom for having the foresight to save her incredible 1960s couture wedding gown for me to wear, and to my mom-in-law, Jane, for knowing how to alter it at the last minute. And, as always, thanks to my lovelies, David and Havana.

# RESOURCES

## DESIGNERS

See a gown that you love in this book? Contact information is listed below for the designers we have featured (see pages 175-176 for designer credits). Please note that the names of bridalwear lines are subject to change. For the most up-to-date wedding gown designs and designer contact information, log on to www.theknot.com/gowns, where thousands of styles are on view 24/7, or contact the showrooms directly.

ALBERTA FERRETI
212.460.5500

ALFRED SUNG
416.247.4628
www.alfredsungbridals.com

ALVINA VALENTA
212.354.6798

AMADINE
818.563.2113

AMY MICHELSON
818.755.1599
www.amymichelson.com

ANNE BARGE
404.230.9995
www.annebarge.com

AVINE PERUCCI
212.932.0249
www.stpucchi.com

BADGLEY MISCHKA
800.786.0903

BAYJE BRIDAL
408.688.0160 or 800.942.7837

BIRNBAUM & BULLOCK
212.242.2914
www.birnbaumandbullock.com

CARMI COUTURE
*This line has been discontinued.*

CAROLINA HERRERA
212.944.5757

CATHERINE REGEHR
604.734.9339
www.catherineregehr.com

CLEA COLET
212.396.4608

COCOE VOCI
310.360.0287
www.cocoevoci.com

COSE BELLE
212.988.4210

CRISTINA ARZUAGA & CO.
212.780.9647

DOMO ADAMI
800.446.4696
www.domoadami.com

EDGARDO BONILLA
856.216.7726 x2 or 877.bonilla

ELIZABETH EMANUEL
212.245.3390

ELIZABETH FILLMORE
212.647.0863

GALINA
212.564.1020
www.galinabridals.com

GINZA/SIGNATURE
DESIGNS/PRIVATE LABEL BY G
800.858.3338
www.privatelabelbyg.com

GIORGIO ARMANI
212.209.3522

HOUSE OF BIANCHI
800.669.2346

INES DI SANTO
905.856.9115

JANELL BERTÉ
717.291.9894
www.berte.com

JENNIFER TISCORNIA
973.890.8616

JESSICA McCLINTOCK
800.333.5301

JIM HJELM COUTURE
800.686.7880

JUSTINA McCAFFREY
888.874.GOWN
www.justinamccaffrey.com

LES NOCES
514.937.5747

L'EZU ATELIER
213.622.2422
www.lezu.com

LILA BROUDÉ
212.921.8081

LOVE ILLUSION
973.844.0582

MANALÉ
877.2manale

MANOLO COLLECTION
212.997.4697

MARIA ROMIA
215.564.1011

MAX CHAOUL
212.245.3390

MELISSA SWEET
404.633.4395
www.melissasweet.com

MERA BY VALERIE MICHELLE
714.826.8266
www.merabride.com

MIA CALLAWAY
404.794.5801
www.mcbridal.com

MIKA INATOME
212.966.7777
www.mikainatome.com

MYRNALIZ SAN MIGUEL
787.642.3648

PETER LANGNER
39.06.807.82.28
www.peterlangner.com

PRONOVIAS
888.776.6684
www.pronovias.com

REEM ACRA
212.414.0980

RENA KOH
561.470.8894

REVA MIVASAGAR
212.334.3860 or 415.981.3301

ROBERT LEGERE
212.631.0606
www.robertlegerebridal.com

SELIA YANG
212.254.9073

TATIANA OF BOSTON
617.262.4914

VAN HERR BRIDAL
213.680.3630

WEARKSTATT
212.334.9494

YOULIN
(FORMERLY WHITE JADE BY YOULIN)
212.563.0659

YUMI KATSURA
212.772.3760

## PROFESSIONAL ORGANIZATIONS

**CFDA**
1412 Broadway, #2006
New York, NY 10018
212.302.1821

*Council of Fashion Designers of
America: a nonprofit organization that
promotes the appreciation of fashion
arts through fashion and awards
shows. Great for show schedules and
background info on designers.*

**FASHION GROUP INTERNATIONAL**
597 Fifth Avenue
New York, NY 10017
212.593.1715
www.fgi.org

*A nonprofit professional organization
for fashion and related fields; provides
timely info regarding national and
global trends.*

**NATIONAL BRIDAL SERVICE**
3122 West Cary Street
Richmond, VA 23221
804.355.6945
www.nationalbridal.com

*An exclusive membership organization
of independently owned businesses
that serve the bridal market. Find out if
your local retailer is a member, or find
a member retailer near you.*

**INTERNATIONAL ASSOCIATION OF
CLOTHING DESIGNERS**
475 Park Avenue South, Ninth Floor
New York, NY 10016
212.685.6602

*An organization that provides
information on clothing designers—
bios, show schedules—and executives.*

**NEW YORK FASHION CALENDAR**
153 East 87th Street
New York, NY 10128
212.289.0420

*Daily listings of designer shows
and events.*

## GOWN PRESERVATION

**AMERICAN INSTITUTE FOR
CONSERVATION OF HISTORIC
AND ARTISTIC WORKS**
1717 K Street, NW, Suite 301
Washington, D.C. 20006
202.452-9545

**WEDDING GOWN SPECIALISTS
ASSOCIATION**
454 Old Cellar Road
Orange, CT 06477
800.501.5005
www.weddinggownspecialists.com

**J. SCHEER & CO.**
23 Market Street
Rhinebeck, NY 12572
800.448.7291
www.jscheer.com

**HALLAK CLEANERS**
1232 Second Avenue
New York, NY 10021
888.343.2111

**MADAME PAULETTE**
1255 Second Avenue
New York, NY 11101
877.couture
www.madamepaulette.com

**IMPERIAL GOWN RESTORATION**
2814 Merrilee Drive, Suite C
Fairfax, VA 22031
800.wed.gown
www.gown.com

BIBLIOGRAPHY

Behr, Mitchell. *The Beautiful Bride.* New York: The Berkley Publishing Group, 1998.

Calasibetta, Charlotte Mankey. *Fairchild's Dictionary of Fashion,* 2nd rev. ed. New York: Fairchild Books, 1998.

Chase, Deborah. *Every Bride Is Beautiful.* New York: William Morrow and Company, 1999.

Cole, Harriet. *Jumping the Broom: The African-American Wedding Planner.* New York: Henry Holt, 1995.

Costa, Shu Shu. *Wild Geese and Tea: An Asian-American Wedding Planner.* New York: Riverhead Books, 1997.

Cunnington, Phillis, and Catherine Lucas. *Costume for Births, Marriages and Deaths.* New York: Barnes & Noble Books, 1972.

Eicher, Dana Chernoff. *Getting Hitched Without a Hitch: How to Plan Your Dream Wedding in the Real World.* Kansas City: Andrews McMeel Publishing, 1999.

Gordon, Susan J. *Wedding Days: When and How Great Marriages Began.* New York: William Morrow and Company, 1998.

Gorsiline, Douglas. *What People Wore.* New York: Dover Publications, 1980.

Gwynne, J. L. *The Illustrated Dictionary of Lace.* Berkeley, Calif.: LACIS Publications, 1997.

Khalje, Susan. *Bridal Couture: Fine Sewing Techniques for Wedding Gowns and Evening Wear.* Iola, Wis.: Krause Publications, 1997.

Mcbride-Mellinger, Maria. *The Wedding Dress.* New York: Random House, 1993.

———. *The Perfect Wedding.* New York: Collins Publishers, 1997.

Mordecai, Carolyn. *Weddings: Dating and Love Customs of Cultures Worldwide, Including Royalty.* Phoenix: Nittany Publishers, 1999.

Olian, JoAnne. *Wedding Fashions 1862–1912: 380 Costume Designs from "La Mode Illustrée."* New York: Dover Publications, 1994.

Stewart, Arlene Hamilton. *A Bride's Book of Wedding Traditions.* New York: William Morrow and Company, 1995.

Tober, Barbara. *The Bride: A Celebration.* New York: Harry N. Abrams, 1984.

Tottora, Phyllis G., and Robert S. Merkel. *Fairchild's Dictionary of Textiles.* 7th ed. New York: Fairchild Publications, 1996.

Zimmerman, Catherine S. *The Bride's Book: A Pictorial History of American Bridal Gowns.* New York: Arbor House Publishing Co., 1985.

# GOWN CREDITS

Here's a page-by-page list of the gowns that appear throughout the book. Look to the Resources section (pages 168–170) for designers' numbers and Web sites, where applicable. For the most up-to-date wedding gown designs and designer contact information, log on to www.theknot.com/gowns, where thousands of styles are on view 24/7, or contact the showrooms listed in the Resources section.